Getting The Most From Your PC's Hard Disk

C000319298

by
J. W. Penfold

BERNARD BABANI (publishing) LTD
THE GRAMPIANS
SHEPHERDS BUSH ROAD
LONDON W6 7NF
ENGLAND

Please Note

Although every care has been taken with the production of this book to ensure that any projects, designs, modifications and/or programs etc. contained herewith, operate in a correct and safe manner and also that any components specified are normally available in Great Britain, the Publishers and Author do not accept responsibility in any way for the failure, including fault in design, of any project, design, modification or program to work correctly or to cause damage to any other equipment that it may be connected to or used in conjunction with, or in respect of any other damage or injury that may be so caused, nor do the Publishers accept responsibility in any way for the failure to obtain specified components.

Notice is also given that if equipment that is still under warranty is modified in any way or used or connected with home-built equipment then that warranty may be void.

© 1990 BERNARD BABANI (publishing) LTD

First Published — July 1990
Reprinted — March 1993

British Library Cataloguing in Publication Data:
Penfold, J. W.
    Getting the most from your pc's hard disk.
    1. Microcomputer systems. Hard disks
    I. Title
    004.56

    ISBN 0 85934 225 5

Printed and Bound in Great Britain by Cox & Wyman Limited, Reading

Preface

A hard disk is now perhaps the most desired feature of any personal computer. It allows you to have all your application programs and your data files quickly to hand, and allows a quick startup, with no need to shuffle floppy disks in and out of the drive.

For those thinking of adding a hard disk, this book gives the basic information on how a disk is fitted, and how to format it and prepare it for use. The information on interleave factors and installing DOS may also be useful to those who already have a hard disk.

For those with hard disks, this book gives advice on arranging your files in subdirectories so that they are easy to find, and also on making your applications easy to use. Information and advice on backup and security procedures is also included, plus a section with technical details of hard disk operation under DOS.

A hard disk is very much more than a large and fast version of a floppy disk. It needs a wholly different approach to gain most benefit from it. This book will show you how.

J. W. Penfold

Notice

In the example batch files reproduced in this book, some lines have the ECHO command on its own. This is to produce blank lines on the screen to improve the appearance of the display. These commands must be followed by at least one space. If these lines produce a display of "Echo is on" or "Echo is off" (or similar), it could be that your editor does not permit trailing spaces. In this case, these ECHO commands may be omitted.

Warning

Note that in the U.K. certain upgrades might invalidate the manufacturer's warranty (especially upgrades that involve adding something other than an expansion card to the computer). However, provided you do not damage anything when upgrading a computer, the retailer's guarantee is probably still valid. As manufacturers' guarantees often go beyond the statutory minimum requirements of a retailer's warranty, you might still be losing out to some degree. The law governing guarantees might be different to this in other countries. If a computer has some form of on-site or other maintenance agreement, this might also be affected by upgrades. It is advisable to read the "small print" in the agreement before proceeding with any upgrade. If you are in any doubt it is best to first check with the retailer and/or manufacturer.

Trademarks

Contents

Page

Chapter 1
FITTING A HARD DISK 1
How Big? 1
Disk Installation 2
The Disk Drive 2
Types of Fitting 3
Will it Fit? 5
Electrical Connections 7
Controller Cards 8
MFM and RLL 9
Interface Standards 10
Data Connections 11
Fitting the Hard Disk 13
Fitting the Controller Card 15

Chapter 2
HARD DISK FORMATTING 19
Low-Level Formatting 20
Tracks and Sectors 20
AT Setup Step 21
The Formatting Program 22
Interleave Factor 24
Bad Tracks 25
High-Level Formatting 26
Partition Sizes 28
Using FORMAT 30
Extended Partitions 30
High-Level Formatting — DRDOS 30
Changing the Active Partition 32
Booting Up from the Hard Disk 32
Configuring Your System 33
CONFIG.SYS 33
AUTOEXEC.BAT 35

Chapter 3
HARD DISK FILE MANAGEMENT 37
Hierarchical Filing System 37
The Root Directory 38

Chapter 3 (Continued)
Subdirectories 40
Creating and Using Subdirectories 42
MKDIR 42
CHDIR 43
RMDIR 44
The TREE Command 45
Floating Drives 46
Running Applications in Subdirectories 47
The PATH Command 48
The APPEND Command 51
Disk Management 52

Chapter 4
SECURITY AND BACKUP PROCEDURES 57
Backup Methods 57
Backup Programs 58
The Archive Attribute 60
The Backup Operation 60
The BACKUP Command 62
BACKUP Log Files 64
RESTORE Programs 65
Backup Policy 66
XCOPY 68
Preserving Your Hard Disk Contents 71

Chapter 5
ADVANCED USERS SECTION 73
Batch Files 73
Passing Parameters 73
File Renaming in Batch Files 75
Changing the PATH Setting 77
Subdirectories and SUBST 78
More on IF 79
Branching in Batch Files 81
Using CHKDSK 82
Data Allocation and Files 86
DOS Disk Structure 87

Index 89

Chapter 1

FITTING A HARD DISK

In the early days of home computing, it was often said that real computing started when a disk drive was bought. Now, much the same might be said about hard disks. A hard disk allows you to start up at the beginning of the day by just switching on the computer. The operating system, tailored to your requirements, will boot automatically, and you are ready to begin entering commands. All your applications and data files are ready to hand, and you can switch from job to job quickly and easily. The convenience a hard disk provides cannot be over-estimated.

How Big?
The earliest hard disks were of 5 and 10 megabytes (mb) capacity. At that time, 64 kilobytes (k) was felt to be adequate memory, and such disks were considered huge. Now, even 20mb is felt to be a modest size hard disk, and the most common sizes fitted in new computers are 32 and 40mb. There is good reason for this, as applications are growing in size all the time, and consist of ever-increasing numbers of executable and configuration files. dBASE IV, for example, can take up to 5mb of hard disk space, even before you create any data files. DTP programs can create data files which can be several hundred kilobytes in length, especially if scanned graphics are used.

If you are only going to use a computer for word processing, with perhaps a few games and a graphics program, 20mb might prove perfectly adequate, and such drives are now available for very reasonable prices. 32mb is a good size if you want to avoid complications, as most versions of DOS (all except DOS 4 and DRDOS) can only handle drives larger than this by splitting them into two or more smaller "logical" drives.

If you can handle a split drive, or if you have DOS 4/DRDOS, 40mb is a good size for an individual user.

It should take all the applications you should ever want to use, and still leave plenty of space for your data files. A disk of 50—80mb could be advisable if you are planning to generate a very large database, do a lot of DTP work, use scanner graphics, or a combination of these. Larger disks are available, up to the thousands of megabytes, but these are normally only used in large multiuser systems. They are, naturally, very expensive and often need special interfaces.

Generally, the price per megabyte of storage falls as the size of the disk increases. It is therefore better to buy a large drive in the first place, rather than have to add a second at a later date. However, if necessary, it is possible to have more than one hard disk in a computer.

Disk Installation
A hard disk installation in a computer consists of two parts, the drive itself and the controller or interface card. In the case of "hard cards", these two parts are integrated into one physical unit for easy fitting.

The Disk Drive
The drive itself is a sealed metal box, contained in some form of frame or chassis for mounting, with various sockets for attaching leads, and usually several labels giving information about the drive and warning you not to open the case. Inside this case, the actual disk consists in fact of several disks or platters. There may only be one in some drives, but normally there are between two and eight.

The disks are made of aluminium, and are about 3mm thick. They are coated with a layer of magnetic oxide, or the more recent "plated" coating, which is thinner and smoother. Disks are coated on both sides. There is one read/write head for each disk surface. These heads "fly" over the disk surface on a thin film of air which is generated by the rapid rotation of the disk (normally in the region of 3600rpm). Because this film is very thin, it is essential that there is no dust within the case. A dust particle on the disk would cause the head to jump up, and then crash down on the disk, probably scratching it and thereby destroying data. It would not do the head a lot of good either. This is the reason for the sealed case and the warning notices.

Any repair to the inside of a disk drive needs a special "clean room" with filtered dust-free air, and technicians in "space suits". Such facilities are expensive to build and run, and this means that repairs to the smaller sizes (capacities) of hard disks can be uneconomic. It is usually cheaper to simply replace a damaged unit.

The heads are moved across the disk surface by some form of actuator. In the less expensive drives this is done by a stepper motor. In the more expensive types a voice-coil actuator is used. The latter is faster and quieter in operation, but also more expensive. If your drive has a quoted average access time of 65 or 40ms, it is probably a stepper motor type. If the access time is 28ms or less, it is probably a voice-coil type. As well as being faster in operation, voice-coil actuators are also considerably quieter as they step from track to track.

The stepper motor works in fixed steps, and therefore places the tracks at fixed points across the disk surfaces. As the disk drive warms up, the disk expands. Sufficient tolerance is built into the drive to allow for this expansion over a fixed range of operating temperatures. If the drive is allowed to overheat, or become too cold, problems can occur. The voice coil type do not have fixed track positions. Instead, they use one disk surface as a reference, and record markers on this to indicate the track positions. This is reliable over a wider range of temperatures, and also allows the tracks to be closer spaced. It also explains why voice-coil type drives always have an odd number of disk surfaces available for data.

Types of Fitting
There are three ways to fit a hard disk to an IBM PC or compatible computer (referred to in this book as PCs). They are internal, external, and as a hard card.

When a computer is supplied with a hard disk fitted, it is almost invariably fitted internally. This means that it occupies a disk drive "bay" in the computer case, and depending on the design of the case, the front of the drive may become part of the front panel of the case. Normally a "controller card" for the disk drive will occupy one of the expansion slots on the computer motherboard, though some computer motherboards now have the disk drive controllers integrated into them.

An external disk drive is in a separate box to the main computer, and may have its own power supply. It is connected to the computer by a data cable, and will have some form of interface card within the computer. External disk drives are not widely used in the PC world, though quite freely obtainable. They are perhaps mostly used in conjunction with portable or laptop computers, or where it is desired to transport the hard disk, either for use with different computers or for security purposes.

Hard cards consist of a controller card and a hard disk drive in one unit. They are fitted simply by plugging the card into one of the computer's expansion slots. The slot used should be chosen with care. Adequate ventilation must be ensured to prevent the drive overheating, and so the slot used should normally be the one nearest the ventilation slots, or the fan, if fitted. Hard cards are the easiest way of adding a hard disk to a computer not originally fitted with one. It is sometimes said that hard cards are slower in operation than internal hard disks, though it is hard to see why this should be so.

There are also removable hard disks. With these, a mounting rack is fitted in the disk drive bay, and the actual hard disk is slotted into this rack from the front, making the electrical/electronic connections as it does so. The advantage of this system is that it allows the disk to be fitted into more than one machine, perhaps one in the office and one at home. It also allows the disk to be removed for security reasons, perhaps to be stored in a safe or strongroom overnight, or indeed to allow different disks to be fitted into one computer. The various products in this line differ in how much of the drive electronics is removable and how much remains in the computer.

4

A recent development in this line allows almost any 3.5 inch drive to be used as a removable drive in a 5.25 inch bay. It is important, however, to make sure the drive is sufficiently robust to take regular removal and transportation in this way. Some very recent drives are described as "self-parking" and these are often the best type to use.

Will it Fit?

The first consideration when fitting a hard disk is obviously to make sure there is space for it. Internal hard disks fit in the disk drive bays within the case, which also take the floppy disk drives. Fitting a hard disk therefore reduces the number of floppy disk drives you can have by one. This is rarely a problem as a system with one hard disk and one floppy disk is perfectly workable, and in fact is probably the most common configuration. Most computer cases have three or four disk drive bays anyway.

There are three aspects to the physical size of a hard disk drive. Firstly, the size of the actual disk, the "platter"; secondly, the size of the frame it is mounted in; and thirdly, the height of the drive.

Disk sizes are the same as for floppy disks, either 3.5 inches or 5.25 inches in diameter. One point to watch, however, is that some 3.5 inch drives come in 5.25 inch frames, and therefore fit in a 5.25 inch disk drive bay. Older PC cases often only have 5.25 inch disk bays, and to fit a hard disk to one of these you must make sure it is either a 5.25 inch drive, or a 3.5 inch in a 5.25 inch frame. More recent cases often have a combination of 3.5 inch and 5.25 inch bays, and here it is a case of ensuring that the drive is the right size to fit one of the available bays. Note that you cannot assume that a 3.5 inch floppy disk drive is necessarily occupying a 3.5 inch bay, as these are also sometimes supplied in 5.25 inch frames!

There is little to choose between 3.5 and 5.25 inch drives as regards performance, though it is sometimes said that the smaller drives are faster. However, the smaller drives are in some cases of more modern design, and may have side advantages, such as lower power consumption (therefore being less inclined to overheat), and quieter running. If you want a very large capacity drive, this may limit your choice to 5.25 inch units.

Drives come in half-height, full height, and, in the case of drives of large capacity, double height or higher. Half-height drives are the most common nowadays, and many disk drive bays only have sufficient depth to take this type. If you want to fit a full-height drive, it may be possible if you have two empty bays one above the other, in which case the drive will fill the two bays. Not all case designs allow this, however. Some hard cards use one-third height drives, and in some cases with these, it is possible to use a full-length card in the adjacent slot, though this might cause cooling problems.

All the physical fittings should be supplied either with the drive or as part of the case. Drives are mounted using four screws in the sides of the frame. Make sure these screws are supplied with the drive, as they are normally not a standard thread, and can also vary from manufacturer to manufacturer.

In the case of computers which are in cases made of plastic rather than metal, the drives may first have to be fitted into metal sleeves or boxes. This is necessary to screen the drives from the rest of the computer, and the rest of the computer from the drives. Without this screening, data transfer may be unreliable. Such boxes for empty bays are not normally supplied with the computer, and may be hard to obtain separately. If you are replacing a second floppy disk with a hard disk, you can use the box which held the floppy drive.

Hard cards fit in a full-length expansion slot. Because of the depth of even a half-height drive, most actually take up two slots, the exceptions being those using one-third height drives. As the thickest part of the card is at the end away from the connections, however, it is sometimes possible to put a short or half-length card in the adjacent slot. As mentioned above, the slot used must be chosen to ensure adequate ventilation to the disk drive. Hard cards always use 3.5 inch drives, but even so there are some low-profile cases now available which do not have sufficient depth to take a hard card. If you have a low-profile system unit, you should check on this point before ordering a hard card.

Electrical Connections

The power supply fitted to a PC will normally have sufficient power supply leads for all the drive bays in the case. You should find a bunch of loose leads not going anywhere when you open the case. There are two types of power plug. The original large sort is used on 5.25 inch floppy and hard drives, and the smaller and more recent sort, resembling a telephone plug, is used for 3.5 inch drives (or smaller types). However, adaptors are available, and may be supplied with drives. Some 3.5 inch drives mounted in 5.25 inch frames are already adapted to the larger type of plug.

You should look on the power supply for any indication that one of the output leads may have a higher power rating than the others. If there is such an indication, use the higher rated lead for the hard drive. Unfortunately, though many power supplies do have such a higher-rated output, but often there is nothing at all to indicate which lead it is! No great disaster is likely if you cannot identify a higher rated output, however, especially with a drive of recent design. Some modern 3.5 inch hard disks actually draw less current than ancient 5.25 inch floppy drives, though of course the floppies do not draw power all the time.

It is common to fit 120 or 150 watt power supplies to XT type 8088 or 8086 based computers, 200 watt power supplies to AT type 80286 based machines, and 220 watt supplies to 80386 "power platforms". However, it is much more the number of disk drives to be fitted which should dictate the size of power supply. 150 watts is perfectly adequate for any machine with just one or two drives. If you intend fitting three or four drives, you need a 200 watt supply, and if more than one is to be a hard disk, 220 watts is sensible.

If you feel the power supply in your computer is inadequate for all the drives you would like to fit, it is possible to fit another power supply unit, but you must be careful

7

to make sure that the replacement is both the right size and shape, and has the power switch in the right place. There are quite a number of styles currently in use.

Hard disks actually draw most power on initial switch-on, when the disk is accelerating to working speed. When you switch on a computer with hard disk, it is not unusual for the room lights to dim! If you fit several hard disks to a machine and, on switching on, there is a pop and the machine goes dead, it means that the power supply overload protection has been tripped. The only solution to this is to reduce the number of drives, fit lower consumption drives, or increase the rating of the power supply.

Controller Cards
The controller card is the data interface between the hard disk drive and the computer. For historical reasons, controller cards for XT type and AT type computers are very different, and cannot be interchanged between these machines.

When the original IBM PC was introduced, hard disks were exceedingly expensive and exceedingly large, and no direct provision for fitting one was included in the design. The hard disk controller card for the descendants of this model therefore has to include a ROM BIOS to provide the necessary services. When the AT computer was introduced, provision for hard disk drives was included in the computer's BIOS. There is therefore no BIOS in an AT controller card.

XT controller cards are available for controlling one or two hard disks. There are two possible addresses which the ROM BIOS on the card may occupy, at segment C800 or CA00 hex., and since each BIOS may control one or two drives, this sets a limit of four drives which may be fitted. There is usually a switch (called a DIP switch) or jumpers on the card, which are used to set which address it occupies. Hard cards must also occupy one of these addresses, so the limit of four drives includes any hard card fitted. (It is unusual to fit this many drives as for example, it is much cheaper to have one 40mb drive than two 20mb ones, quite apart from the initial power surge problem mentioned above.)

AT controller cards are very frequently designed as both floppy and hard disk controllers, and may have provision for controlling up to two of each type. The maximum number of drives you can have in an AT type machine depends on the design of the computer BIOS. However, it is most commonly four, as for PC types, and again this includes any hard cards.

For both PC and AT type computers, controllers for hard disks only are usually short or half length cards. Controllers for both hard and floppy drives will normally be full length cards. Special "cache" or "1:1 Interleave" controller cards for AT/386 computers will also be full-length, even if they are hard disk only controllers.

MFM and RLL

There are two main systems for data encoding currently in use on hard disks. These are known by the initials MFM, which stands for Modified Frequency Modulation, and RLL, which stands for Run Length Limited. The exact meaning of these two terms need not concern the user, but basically RLL (which in fact is a form of MFM) is used to record data on to a drive in a more compact form. This gives a drive of a given size a greater storage capacity, and may also give a higher data transfer rate.

There is some controversy surrounding RLL cards. Some card manufacturers say you can use RLL cards with any drive, but drive manufacturers tend to insist that they should only be used with drives intended for them, specificially described as RLL drives. It seems that if an RLL card is used with an MFM drive, all may seem to work well at first, but after six months or so, you may have difficulty reading back data previously saved. According to some experts, however, this can happen even when using an RLL card with an RLL drive.

The cause of the problem is said to be interference with the signal being sent from the hard disk during accesses. This is somewhat weaker than the signal from an MFM drive because of the higher data density. Problems are more likely to occur in a "noisy" electrical environment.

This means anywhere where other electrical equipment (other computers, photocopiers, fax machines) is in use. In a quieter environment, RLL may prove perfectly reliable. Having a good earth connection may also help. Note that even at home, fridges, microwave ovens and vacuum cleaners (among other things) can cause a lot of electrical "noise".

The best advice is probably only to use RLL cards with RLL drives, and MFM cards with MFM drives. If you are very concerned about data security, you will probably want to stick to MFM. However, there is a very significant price advantage to using the RLL system, as a 32mb RLL drive is only around the same price as a 21mb MFM drive. RLL is also anything up to 50% faster in transferring data. RLL does seem to be gradually taking over, and some manufacturers now only make RLL equipment.

Interface Standards

Until quite recently, nearly all controller cards and hard disks used a single interface standard, known as ST506, because this was the type number of the original controller card using it. Another popular card type, ST412, uses the same standard, which is therefore sometimes just called "ST". Both the MFM and RLL cards mentioned above use this standard. However, this standard has its limitations in data transfer speed, and trying to increase that speed, as has been done with RLL for instance, tends to reduce reliability.

Two other standards have recently started to become available for PC type computers. These are ESDI and SCSI.

ESDI has a certain amount in common with the ST standard, and the data connections are very similar. However, the difference is that more of the work of translating the data from the computer to signals on the disk, and back again, is done in the disk circuitry, and less on the controller card. This allows a considerably improved data transfer rate, compared with the ST standard. It should also give greater reliability, as the signal sent along the data cable can be stronger.

SCSI is quite different. It is not just a system for connecting hard disks, but a form of fast serial interface by which other devices, such as scanners, can also be connected to the computer. As a means of connecting a hard disk, it allows very much faster data transmission than either ST or ESDI.

Unfortunately, SCSI is not a rigorously enforced single standard. There are many slight variants on it. This means that it is not at present the versatile system for attaching peripherals that it might be. There have recently been moves to create a new, stricter standard, to be called SCSI II (or SCSI2), and it is to be hoped this will be successful.

Both these new interface standards are at present very much more expensive than ST. The interfaces and hard disks are also more difficult to find, though becoming more available all the time. As always, you must take care to ensure that you buy a disk and an interface card which do match. With SCSI in particular, there are differing approaches. You can buy SCSI controller cards which are for hard disks (or hard and floppy) only, or you can buy SCSI cards which are for interfacing any SCSI device. You may need an additional adaptor card to use these with a hard disk.

These systems are also only really worth considering if you have a fastish computer. They would not be of great benefit as an update to a PC XT or slow AT. They may be worth considering if you have a fast AT or an 80386 machine, and you do a lot of disk intensive work, for instance with a database, DTP or CAD program.

Data Connections

There are normally two data leads running between the controller card and each hard disk. These are both of the ribbon cable type, and one is much wider than the other. The wide, 34-pin cable is called the control lead, and the narrower, 20-pin cable is the data lead proper. There are exceptions to this. Some Xebec drives use only a single data lead. These drives can only be used with the card specifically designed for them and not with other cards, and in fact use a different interface standard, SASI, a fore-runner of SCSI. These drives are rare, but were fitted to early Amstrad PC1512 computers. SCSI cards and drives also differ in their connections. As with power leads, there are differences between the plugs for 5.25 and 3.5 inch drives, but 3.5 inch drives in 5.25 inch frames may use the 5.25 inch type.

With the narrower lead, you have a completely separate lead for each drive. With the wider lead, however, one lead goes to the two drives, and it therefore has three plugs on it (one for the card, two for the drives). As supplied, the leads are normally quite long, but with the dual drive lead, there is sometimes not very much lead between the two drive plugs. You may need to check that the two drives are mounted close enough in the case for the lead to stretch between them. They may need to be one above the other, rather than side by side.

This dual lead introduces a strange quirk in hard disk installation. On each drive, there is a switch which sets whether the drive is the first or the second on the control-ler card. However, for PCs, this switch is always set to the "first drive" position, regardless of whether the drive is actually being used as the first or the second. The second drive is set by having a "twist" in the cable between the first and the second drives. That is to say, the connections between pins 24 to 28 to the second drive are reversed. Therefore, the drive connected to the plug without the twist will be Drive C, and the drive connected to the plug with the twist will be Drive D, assuming that the card in question is controlling the first two hard disks, if there are more than two, and that neither hard disk has been parti-tioned. (Partitioning is discussed in a later chapter.) The plug without the twist will not necessarily be the first on the lead.

There is also a setting which needs to be made on the actual disk drive. Each disk is supplied with a "terminat-ing resistor pack" fitted. This will be a long cylindrical object somewhere on the outside of the case. If fitting only a single drive, this should be left in place. If fitting two drives on a lead, it should be removed from the first drive.

It seems to be normal practice for the connecting leads to be supplied with the controller card rather than with the disk drive. Some suppliers, however, price drive, controller and cables as three separate items. You may need to specify that you want leads to connect two drives, especially if you are buying a drive and controller card together. Other suppliers always supply the leads for two drives. If catalogue information is unclear or incomplete, it never hurts to check before placing an order.

Fitting the Hard Disk
As fitting a hard disk involves opening the case, the first thing to do is to ensure that the computer is switched off and disconnected from the mains, and from any peripherals such as printers. In fact, there should not be any mains voltages outside the power supply unit, but better safe than sorry. The second thing you should do is note down any information on the labels which may be needed during formatting. This includes any details of the number of tracks and cylinders on the drive, and the positions of any bad tracks found during factory testing.

There are a great many styles and types of PC case in use today, and since details of how to fit drives into them can vary quite widely, it would probably be counter-productive to try to describe the process in detail. The method of fitting is usually quite obvious once you have examined the case and the drive chassis. One important point, however, is the difference between cases intended for PC type computers and those intended for AT types.

In cases intended for PC motherboards, the disk drives normally bolt directly into the case. With AT type cases, you also need special plastic strips or "rails". These are bolted onto the disk drive. The drive can then be slid into the case from the front. There is normally also some method of locking the drive into position in the case once fitted. If you specifically order a disk drive for an AT type computer, it should come with the rails. However, AT cases often come complete with a set of rails for each drive bay already in place.

As mentioned earlier, some plastic cased computers require the drive to be fitted first into a metal screening box. This box is then fitted into the case. It is essential that the box is used if data transfer is to be reliable, and in any case the drive will not normally fit without it. However, if you buy the computer with only a single floppy drive, the metal box may not be fitted, and it may be hard to obtain it separately. The most common computer of this type is the Amstrad PC1512, and you may find hard disk "kits" advertised for this computer which include all the necessary bits. If not, it is not difficult for a handyman to fabricate a suitable box from thin aluminium sheet.

The sizes of hard disk drive chassis are well standardised, and it is extremely unusual to find that a drive cannot be fitted within a case. This is only likely to happen if you have bought a very non-standard disk drive, as can happen if you shop at a computer auction. This is a very bad place to buy a hard disk! Not only are drives likely to be odd-balls, but they are also likely to be incorrectly described (e.g. a 40mb drive turning out to be an ancient 5mb variety), faulty or thoroughly worn out.

Once in place, the connections to the drive may be somewhat inaccessible. This is especially true when the drive is contained in a box. If this looks likely to be the case, fit the leads to the drive before installing it.

It is important that the disk drive is not physically stressed when installed. If the screw positions on the drive do not line up correctly with the holes in the case mounts, enlarge the holes as necessary with a small file, taking care not to allow any of the swarf to remain in the computer case, where it could cause short circuits, or severe physical damage if it got into a floppy disk drive. Hard disks are well sealed, but often part of the mechanism is exposed, and problems could occur here also. If the front of the hard disk also forms part of the front of the case when fitted, it is important that there is no pressure on the drive here either. Ensure that any ventilation slots, especially on the front of the chassis, are not obstructed.

Any stress or pressure on the disk drive chassis can cause the drive to overheat in use. If this happens, data transfer is likely to become unreliable, as the platter will expand beyond the design allowances. This will mean that data recorded when the drive is cold cannot be read back when it is hot, and vice versa. It is also likely to lead to premature failure of the drive. The mounting screws of the drive should also not be over-tightened for this reason. As the vibration of the drive is likely to loosen the screws over a period of time, it is a good idea to put a dab of paint over each one to fix it. This is effective, and does not prevent the drives being removed at a later date if necessary.

Fitting the Controller Card
The controller card is fitted into one of the expansion slots in the computer. You need to check that you have a slot available for the type of card you intend using.

As well as types for PC and AT computers, the differences between which have already been covered, there are other types of card, some of which can only be fitted to specific categories of computers. Micro-channel architecture (MCA) and the forthcoming EISA (not to be confused with ESDI) computers will need cards very different from the current XT/AT types. However, many of these computers have, or will have, the controller circuitry on the motherboard.

As already mentioned, there are half-length and full-length cards for XT and AT computers. The first thing to check is that there is enough physical space for the card. As far as data transfer is concerned, slots can be either 8-bit or 16-bit. PCs only have 8-bit slots. AT and other more advanced types, including "386" and "486" computers, can have a mixture of 8 and 16 bit slots. 386 (but not 386SX) and 486 computers can also have 32-bit slots, and these are compatible with 8-bit slots.

Controller cards for AT computers are always designed to fit a 16-bit slot. This allows a faster data transfer. You should therefore check that you have a suitable 16-bit slot free. 32-bit controllers for 386 and 486 computers are made, and often fitted as original equipment to these computers, but I have yet to see one advertised for sale separately, perhaps because computers of this type are still rare, and are invariably supplied with hard disks fitted. In some cases also, the disk controller for these is integrated onto the motherboard.

You may also see cards described as "Cache" or "1:1 interleave". These allow very fast data transfer, as data is read off the disk and stored on the card until the computer can use it, but are quite expensive, largely because they have a lot of on-board memory. You need a fast computer to take full advantage of one of these cards, but they fit a normal full-length 16-bit slot.

You should receive some form of manual or instruction book with the controller card. If you don't, ask for one. This will give you information on any jumper settings which may need to be altered. On XT cards, you may need to set the address to be used by the controller BIOS, either C800 or CA00 hex. This is only necessary if you have two controllers installed. They obviously cannot occupy the same address space. You may also need to set jumpers to indicate the type of disk drive installed (i.e. number of heads and cylinders, which should be marked on the drive or given in the manual), though some cards allow this information to be keyed in during formatting.

To fit the controller, you must first remove the metal blanking plate from the end of the slot. This blanking plate forms, in effect, part of the outside of the case. You do this by removing the appropriate screw, but it is often hard to tell which screw belongs to which blanking plate, as the screw is in fact to the side of the plate. There may be an impressed arrow on the end of the plate to indicate the right screw.

The card will also have a blanking plate to one end of it, and this is inserted into the space occupied by the removed plate. Push the edge connectors on the card firmly but gently into the expansion slots, but try to keep your fingers off the copper tracks on the card, and also take care not to exert pressure on any of the electronic components on the card. When the controller is installed correctly, replace the screw.

As with the disk drive, it may be difficult to attach the connectors to the card once it is in place. Again, you can

16

attach the leads before installing the card.

Fitting a hard card is essentially similar to fitting a controller card. The only difference is that you need to ensure that there is enough space for the actual drive on the end of the card away from the blanking plate, which may mean that you need to have two spare slots, and that the card is installed in the position which gets the best ventilation. This may entail moving other, previously installed, cards to different slots. Of course, with a hard card, all connections are made through the expansion slot, and there are no leads to connect to the power supply or elsewhere.

Closing the case completes the physical installation. You can now turn the computer on. As soon as power is applied, the disk drive should start to spin. During the computer's start-up sequence, the hard disk access light (on the drive or on the front panel or both) should come on briefly. Depending on the design of the controller card, on PC computers, you may get a "Hard Disk Installed" message. You should not be able to access the hard disk yet, as it has not been formatted. Any attempt to do so should produce the message "Disk (or Drive) Not Ready". However, hard disks are sometimes supplied already formatted.

Hard cards are more often supplied already formatted, and even with some software installed, so at this stage a hard card may be ready to use.

Chapter 2

HARD DISK FORMATTING

Before data can be saved on to a hard disk, it has to be formatted, just like a floppy disk. However, unlike a floppy, this formatting is divided into two stages. These are known as low-level and high-level formatting.

These two stages are necessary because of the mass-storage nature of a hard disk. Whereas a floppy disk can belong exclusively to one operating system, and if you use a second operating system you can use another floppy, a hard disk is a fixed component of a computer. In fact, "fixed disk" is an alternative name for a hard disk. If, therefore, you want to use two or more operating systems, they will need to share the hard disk.

The basic low-level formatting is really a matter between the disk controller and the disk itself. The operating system is interested only in how big the sectors are and how many of them are available. The actual way they are arranged and addressed on the physical disk is not its direct concern. The low-level format can be common to all operating systems which use the disk.

On the other hand, the high level format, the way in which files are arranged on the disk and the way in which the operating system allocates its space, is particular to each operating system. Each operating system on the disk therefore needs to have its own high-level formatting, so this is done separately by a program belonging to that operating system.

The way the disk is divided up between the operating systems, the "partitioning", which is described later, is the link between the common structure and the high-level or logical formatting of each operating system. All systems must recognise the partitioning so that they do not exceed their allotted area of the disk.

Nowadays, it is not common for a PC user to use more than one operating system. Nearly everybody uses some form of DOS, and nothing else. This was not the case in the early days of PCs, when CP/M 86 was commonly used. It may also not be the case in the future, as operating systems such as UNIX and its derivatives are gaining ground fast. Partitioning may become an important feature of hard disk use again.

Partitioning has a second function in allowing one disk to be divided up into two or more "logical" drives which look to DOS like entirely separate disks. This is a way of using hard disks larger than DOS was designed to accommodate, and can also be used as a method of organisation.

Low-Level Formatting — WARNING:
When low-level formatting a hard disk, any existing data on that disk is likely to be destroyed. Before formatting a disk, make sure either that there is no data on the disk, or that you have TWO copies of any data you wish to retain. The Author and Publishers will accept no responsibility for any loss of data or consequential loss occurring as a result of applying the instructions in this book.

Tracks and Sectors
In order to be able to find data on a disk, some form of organisation of the surface is necessary. The surface is mapped into a series of concentric circles, called tracks. Each track is in turn marked into a series of sectors. These are the basic units of storage on the disk. Data is always read and stored in full sectors.

Most hard disks have more than one surface. The number of surfaces is usually indicated as the number of heads. A "cylinder", as used in giving a disk specification, consists of all the tracks for a given head position (the heads always move together) on all the surfaces. The total number of sectors on a hard disk is therefore obtained by the formula

sectors per track X cylinders X heads

The amount of data which a sector can hold varies, but on PCs is nearly always 512 bytes, or ½ kilobyte. If therefore, you divide the total number of sectors by 2, you get the disk capacity in kilobytes, and if you divide this by 1024, you get the capacity in megabytes. For example, my disk has 17 sectors per track, 640 cylinders and 4 heads.

$$17 \times 640 \times 4 = 43520 \text{ (sectors)}$$

$$43520 \div 2 = 21760 \text{ (kb)}$$

$$21760 \div 1024 = 21.25 \text{ (mb)}$$

The purpose of low-level or physical formatting is to record signals on the disk which marks it into tracks and sectors, and which also number the sectors. Dummy data is written into every sector, and low-level formatting therefore destroys any data on the disk.

AT Setup Step

With an AT type computer, there is a preliminary step to be performed before formatting the drive. The set-up program supplied with all AT machines, either on disk or in the BIOS ROM must be used, to tell the operating system that a hard disk is present, and what type it is. The type setting determines how many tracks, and how many sectors on each track, the format program will place on the disk. This sets how much data the drive can have recorded on it.

Often, the drive will have this information on an attached label, together with the position of any bad tracks on the drive which were detected during testing by the manufacturer. You should have made a note of any such data before installing the drive, as suggested in Chapter 1.

The next step is to compare this data with the list of drive types which will normally be included in the computer manual, or in the motherboard manual if you are assembling your own. There is a standard set of drives, as supported by the original IBM PC AT computer, so the first 14 types are often the same. There is, however, much less standardisation for type numbers of 16 and above (type no. 15 is not used), as manufacturers have added types on an ad hoc basis.

21

If you cannot find an exact match for the specification of your drive, all is not lost. You can use the nearest similar specification with the right number of heads but fewer cylinders, or if absolutely essential, the right number of cylinders but fewer heads. This will involve some loss of your disk's capacity — probably more so if you have to set fewer heads than if you have to set fewer cylinders. You should not select a type which has either more heads or more cylinders than your actual drive, as this could obviously cause trouble as the formatting program tries to format non-existent parts of the disk. Having matched your drive with a type number, you enter this number when running the set-up program.

There is no such set-up program with PC computers. The drive type is set either with jumpers or switches on the controller card, as described in Chapter 1, or is keyed in when using the low-level format program.

The Formatting Program
The low-level format program is normally included in the BIOS on PC controller cards, or supplied on disk for AT machines. There are also commercial low-level formatting programs available, for both PC and AT types (but often not interchangeable between the two), which may have advantages over the supplied utilities. The Xebec drives fitted to early Amstrad PC1512s mentioned in Chapter 1 were not supplied with any type of FORMAT program.

To use the BIOS formatting program on a PC, you need to use the DEBUG utility supplied with MS-DOS or PC-DOS. Insert a floppy disk with a copy of DEBUG on it into the current drive, and type DEBUG. You will then see the DEBUG prompt which is a dash. At this prompt, type the following exactly:—

    G=C800:5

On pressing the ENTER key, the formatting program should run. If this does not work, try:—

    G=C800:6

This is an alternative address used by some cards.

Some computers come with a short program, usually called HDFORMAT. This can be used instead of DEBUG to run the BIOS formatting program. Such a program was supplied with the Amstrad PC1512 despite the lack of a BIOS FORMAT. In fact, it caused FDISK (described in the next chapter) to run. However, if you have to replace the Xebec hard disk and controller (apparently not uncommon), HDFORMAT should run the BIOS FORMAT on the new card.

These FORMAT programs do vary in nature, so no detailed instructions can be given here. Generally, though, you will be asked a series of questions, which may include which drive you want to format (only relevant, of course, if you have fitted more than one drive), either the drive type, or number of tracks and sectors to format, if this has not been previously set on the controller with switches or jumpers, and whether or not you want to split the drive. Figure 2.1 shows the screen display of a typical PC XT type format program.

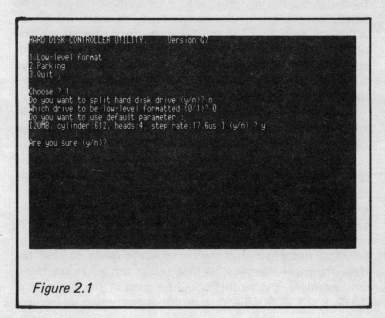

Figure 2.1

Splitting the drive allows you to use a single physical disk drive as if it were two (logical) drives. This may be necessary with very large drives, as versions of MS-DOS and PC-DOS prior to 4.00 cannot handle drives larger than 32mb. Normally at this stage, the drive can only be split into two equal parts. This, for example, will allow a 40mb drive to be used as two 20mb drives. If you fit a drive larger than 64mb you will still not be able to use all the capacity this way. Versions of MS-DOS from 3.3 onward allow the drive to be split at the high-level format stage, and here the split can be unequal. MS-DOS 4.00 onward and DRDOS can handle drives larger than 32mb as single drives.

Interleave Factor
You will almost certainly be asked what interleave factor to use. This is important, as it has a direct bearing on how fast data can be read from and written to the disk. Recently, however, controller cards with fixed interleave factors have been introduced. These are a little cheaper than cards offering selectable interleave. They may be worth considering if you have a fairly standard PC XT or AT type computer, as the fixed settings offered are the ones which are most commonly found to be the best with these. They would not, however, be a good idea with an Amstrad PC1512 or 1640, which often benefit from different settings.

Generally, the computer cannot process data as fast as the drive can read it off the disk. If the sectors on each track were used in physical order, after reading the data in sector 1, the computer could not immediately digest the data off sector 2, so the disk would have to do a full idle rotation before this data could be read. The computer would almost certainly be ready before this, so some time would be wasted.

The idea of interleaving is to number the sectors out of physical order, so that the computer is ready to read the data from a sector just as that sector arrives at the head. For example, the sectors could be used in the order 1, 7, 13, 2, 8, 14, 3, 9, 15 and so on for as many sectors as there are on the disk, normally 17 or 26. This is an interleave factor of 3.

An interleave factor of 3 or 4 is usually the optimum for most PC XT types, with AT type computers working best with 2 or 3. Ideally, the interleave factor should be kept as low as possible for fastest data transfer. However, bear in mind that the worst possible interleave factor is one less than the ideal, so it is better to go for the higher figure if you do not want to experiment with different factors to find the optimum (a time-consuming process, though there are programs which will do it for you). These factors are the ones I have seen offered on fixed-interleave cards.

Some computers, like the Amstrad PC1512s and 1640s, need a much higher interleave factor, usually at least 7 and perhaps as high as 11. If the interleave factor is not set this high, disk drive performance can be very sluggish.

On the 1:1 interleave cards mentioned in Chapter 1, there is enough memory on the card to buffer a complete track of data. This allows data to be read off the hard disk very fast, and stored on the card while the computer digests it. Very high transfer rates are possible with this system, but the high cost of these cards is only worth while with if you have a powerful computer and do a lot of disk-intensive operations (e.g. databases, DTP, CAD).

When you have answered all the questions, the formatting will start. The drive will run, possibly for several minutes, with a rhythmic ticking as the head steps from track to track. Wait patiently until the procedure is complete. You may get a running display of the number of tracks and sectors formatted as the operation proceeds.

Bad Tracks

After the formatting, you get the opportunity to mark the bad tracks listed on the drive label so that they are not used by the computer. It is important to do this, as, although later high-level formatting stages will detect bad sectors, they do not do so with total efficiency. Failing to mark the bad sectors is to risk losing important data at some time in the future.

On some controllers, you will be asked if you want to "Format Bad Tracks". This is confusing, as it sounds as if you are being asked if you want to use these tracks. In fact, the tracks you enter are locked out. You may also be asked if you want to "Set more bad tracks" when in fact you have not yet marked any. This is simply a result of saving space in the BIOS ROM by not having a program sophisticated enough to ask the two questions.

You may find that your hard disk is already formatted when you receive it. Most disks will in fact be formatted as part of factory testing. However, not all controller cards are able to "inherit" format markings from this source. You may still find it worthwhile to format the disk yourself, in order to set the best interleave, and also to set the bad tracks. Though factory formatting is done to find these bad spots, they will not necessarily be "locked out" as part of the process.

High-Level Formatting
When the IBM PC was introduced, several operating systems were offered. Each of these used its own type of directory structure and disk layout. To accommodate these on a single hard disk, a system of partitioning was developed, so that each operating system had its own section of the disk.

You still need to create a DOS partition on a hard disk, even though, for most users, it will be the only partition and will occupy the entire disk. The program to create the partition is FDISK and is supplied as part of the operating system utilities.

FDISK is a menu driven program. Figure 2.2 shows the initial FDISK screen for MS-DOS 3.3, and Figure 2.3 the same for DRDOS 3.41. The menu operations displayed when the program is run will vary, depending on your particular set-up. When using it for the first time, the only options you can choose are to create a DOS partition, or to change to another fixed disk if you have two or more. If you split the disk at the low-level format stage, FDISK will see it as two disks.

FDISK will offer the option it thinks you are most likely to need. To accept this choice, you just press

```
Fixed Disk Setup Program Version 3.30
(C)Copyright Microsoft Corp. 1987

FDISK Options

Current Fixed Disk Drive: 1

Choose one of the following:

    1. Create DOS partition
    2. Change Active Partition
    3. Delete DOS partition
    4. Display Partition Information



Enter choice: [1]



Press ESC to return to DOS
```

Figure 2.2

```
FDISK R1.41    Fixed Disk Maintenance Utility
Copyright (c) 1986,1988 Digital Research Inc. All rights reserved.

Partitions on 1st hard disk (20.2 Mb, 611 cylinders):
No  Drive  Start  End   MB    Status  Type
 1    C:     0    638  21.2    A    DOS 3.0





Select options:
1) Create DOS partition
2) Delete DOS partition
3) Select bootable partition

Enter desired option: (ESC = exit) [?]
```

Figure 2.3

27

ENTER. The choice which should be offered, and which you should take, will normally be no. 1., "Create DOS partition" (see Figure 2.4).

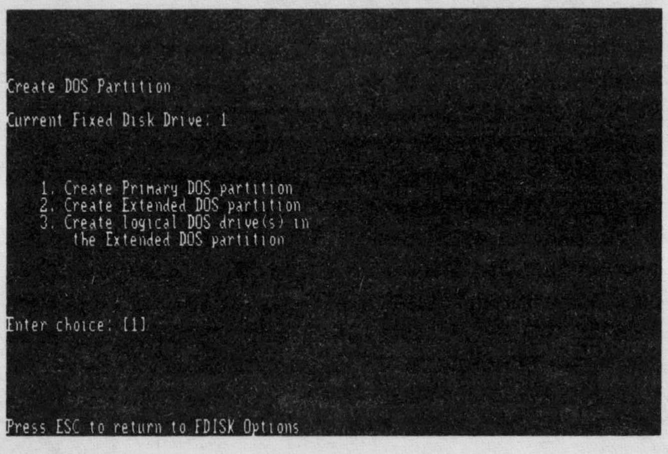

```
Create DOS Partition

Current Fixed Disk Drive: 1


    1. Create Primary DOS partition
    2. Create Extended DOS partition
    3. Create logical DOS drive(s) in
       the Extended DOS partition



Enter choice: [1]



Press ESC to return to FDISK Options
```

Figure 2.4

FDISK will display the number of cylinders available on the disk, and will ask if you want to use the whole disk for DOS. Normally, unless your disk is larger than 32mb, this will be the sensible choice. If you have a disk which is larger than 32mb and this is all your version of DOS can support, the partition size suggested will be only enough cylinders so that the limit is not exceeded.

Partition Sizes
If you want to create a partition which is less than the whole disk, you must specify the size of the partition you want to create in terms of cylinders. Partitioning of the disk is an actual physical dividing up of the space on the disk. To calculate how many cylinders you need to create a partition of a particular size in megabytes, you need to use the following formula:—

$$(\text{size in mb} \times 1048567) \div$$

$$(\text{bytes per sector} \times \text{sectors} \times \text{heads})$$

where "sectors" means the number of sectors per track.

For example, to create a partition of 15mb (as near as possible) on a disk with 512 bytes per sector, 17 sector per track, four heads,

$$15 \times 1048567 \div 512 \times 17 \times 4$$

$$= 15728640 \div 34816$$

$$= 451.76471$$

As you can only set the partition in full cylinders, you would have to choose either 451 or 452.

Depending on the version you have, you may be prompted to enter the number of cylinders you wish to use (which must not be more than the number of cylinders available, which is displayed), or you may be prompted to enter the starting and end cylinders of the portion of the disk you require. Obviously, this cannot overlap with any part of the disk which is already assigned. When you press ENTER after entering the required data, the partition is created.

At this point, the behaviour of MS-DOS/PC-DOS and DRDOS differ. MS/PC-DOS is described here. DRDOS has a section to itself later in the chapter.

Once you have created the partition, FDISK will display a message to the effect that the system will restart. You have to insert a system disk in drive A and press a key. The operating system then reboots.

With MS-DOS version 3.21 and earlier, only a single partition with a maximum size of 32mb can be used for DOS. If your disk is larger than this, you will either need a special program to allow the remainder of the disk to be accessed as a second partition (some manufacturers provide these), or a controller of the type which allows a drive to be split at the low-level format stage. With one of these, you need to use FDISK once on each logical drive.

When FDISK creates the partition, it is automatically made active. This means that data can be stored on it, and also that the system files can be copied on to it.

Using FORMAT

The final stage of formatting with PC-DOS and MS-DOS is to use the FORMAT program, as used to format floppy disks. On a hard disk, this simply creates an empty file allocation table and the root directory. If you specify the /S parameter, the system files will be copied onto the hard disk, so that you can boot up from it, as long as the DOS partition remains the active one.

If you do not specify the /S switch when using FORMAT, you can put the system files on the disk with the SYS command. However, you must do this before saving anything else onto the disk, as the system files must occupy the sectors at the very beginning of the partition. The operating system cannot boot up if they are anywhere else.

Extended Partitions

With MS-DOS 3.3 and higher, you can create primary and extended DOS partitions. You can create an extended DOS partition in any part of the disk not used for the primary partition. This extended partition, which can be greater than 32mb, can be used as one or more logical drives, each of which will have its own drive letter. The maximum size for each logical drive remains 32mb. You must use FORMAT on each of these additional drives before you can save data onto them. You can create only one primary partition, and this is the only DOS partition which can be made active, and therefore the only one from which DOS can be booted. Figure 2.5 shows the FDISK display of partition data on a 40mb disk, under DOS 3.3.

Having completed these stages, the hard disk is now read for use.

High-Level Formatting — DRDOS

DRDOS is an advanced version of DOS from Digital

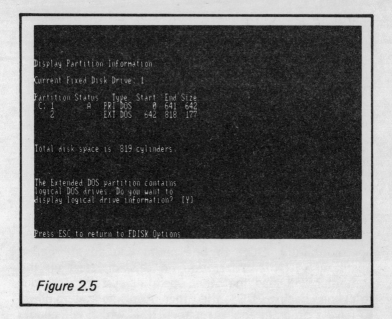

```
Display Partition Information

Current Fixed Disk Drive: 1

Partition Status   Type  Start  End  Size
C: 1        A   PRI DOS    0   641  642
   2            EXT DOS  642   818  177



Total disk space is  819 cylinders.


The Extended DOS partition contains
logical DOS drives. Do you want to
display logical drive information?  [Y]


Press ESC to return to FDISK Options
```

Figure 2.5

Research. Many areas have been improved to make it easier to use, and this includes the high-level formatting of a hard disk.

Whereas MS-DOS uses two programs in order to perform the high-level format, FDISK and FORMAT, in DRDOS FDISK does it all. In fact, if DRDOS detects an unformatted hard disk is present during boot up, it will actually ask you if you want it formatted and start FDISK for you!

Like MS-DOS 3.3, DRDOS can create primary and extended DOS partitions, and allows a single disk to be used as a number of logical drives. However, DRDOS does not have the 32mb limit. It can handle partitions up to 512mb.

The procedure for using FDISK is much like the MS-DOS version, but when creating the primary partition it creates the FAT and main directory automatically, and will transfer the system files if required. It also creates the FAT and directory for any logical drives created in an extended partition. As with other versions of DOS, you have to restart the system after using FDISK.

With DRDOS, FORMAT is never used on a hard disk. If you attempt to use it, you will be told to use FDISK instead. Therefore, with DRDOS, once you have used FDISK your hard disk is ready for use.

A major difference with DRDOS is that the system files can be anywhere on the disk, they do not have to be at the very beginning as in MS-DOS, provided they are in the root directory. SYS can therefore be used anytime to make a disk bootable (hard or floppy). This explains how it is possible for DRDOS to be installed, replacing MS-DOS, without having to reformat the disk.

Changing the Active Partition

If you have two operating systems on your hard disk, FDISK allows you to change the active partition from the one containing DOS to one containing an alternative operating system. After you do this, on start up the computer will load the other operating system. In order to change back to DOS, the other operating system needs to have a program equivalent to FDISK which will enable you to switch the active partition back to the DOS one.

FDISK also includes a facility to delete the DOS partitions. You can delete the extended partition to make room for another operating system, but this will mean losing any data in that partition. It can also delete the DOS primary partition if you no longer want to use the hard disk for DOS. You cannot delete the primary partition while an extended DOS partition exists. You also cannot use FDISK to delete a partition which belongs to another operating system.

Note that when talking about other operating systems, this means systems like CP/M 86, P/System or UNIX/XENIX, and not different versions of DOS. PC-DOS, MS-DOS, and DRDOS are all versions of DOS, and you cannot have two of these on the same hard disk.

Booting Up from the Hard Disk

When you have an active DOS partition on your hard disk, and the system files installed on it, you can boot up DOS from the disk at switch-on automatically. To do this, there must *not* be a disk in drive A. When started, the computer will first go through its diagnostic checks, memory, etc. It will then check for the presence of any additional ROM BIOSs present. It is at this stage that you may see a message "1 hard disks installed" (or more).

The computer will then attempt to boot an operating system. It will first check for the presence of a disk in drive A. If one is present it will attempt to boot the OS from this disk. If the disk in drive A does not have system files present, the message "Wrong disk — Insert a system disk in drive A and press any key" will be displayed. In fact, if you remove the disk from drive A and leave the drive empty, the computer will proceed as in the next paragraph.

If there is no disk in drive A, the computer will attempt to boot the OS from the active partition on the hard disk. If there are no system files in the active partition, or for some reason they are not readable (corruption, hardware fault) you will be prompted to insert a system disk in drive A, and the computer will attempt to boot from that.

The reason the computer will always attempt to boot from a disk in drive A before attempting to boot from the hard disk is so that you may load an alternative operating system without having to change the active hard disk partition with FDISK and then reboot, or so that you may load an operating system should a problem arise with the hard disk.

Configuring Your System
After booting up, the operating system will look in the root directory of the drive for two special files, CONFIG. SYS and AUTOEXEC.BAT. These files can be used when booting from hard or floppy disks, but they are especially valuable when booting automatically from a hard disk, as they allow the operating system to be tailored to your particular needs.

CONFIG.SYS.
The two files have quite different uses. CONFIG.SYS is similar to a batch file, but it does not contain normal

batch file commands. Instead, it contains various device drivers and configuration commands. The commands which can be used in CONFIG.SYS can *only* be used in CONFIG.SYS, and they can also only be used once at the beginning of a session. Many of these commands assign memory to the operating system for special purposes. Others do such things as setting the computer to work using the date format, character set, etc., for a particular country. We will look here at three which have special relevance to hard disk operation, as they affect file handling.

DOS has a limit to the number of files that can be open at once. This limit, however, is variable and can be set according to user requirements in the CONFIG.SYS file. The command is

FILES=nn

where nn is the maximum number of files which can be open at once. Each file needs a certain amount of memory space, and this leaves less memory for use by applications. Applications like databases may need to have a lot of files open at once. On the other hand, programs like DTP may need the maximum of free memory. The number you enter for FILES may need to be a compromise between these two requirements. On most versions of DOS, the smallest value for FILES is 20, and the highest 255. It is sometimes recommended that you should only increase the number from 20 if you use a particular application which demands it.

When a file is open, DOS tries to keep part of it in a memory area called a buffer. It is much faster to read file data from the buffer than to read it from the disk each time it is needed. You can set the number of buffers you have available in CONFIG.SYS. Again, each buffer takes up some memory space, so having more than necessary could give some applications problems. The smallest number of buffers you can normally have is 2 and the highest 99. The most popular compromise is 15. The format of the command is

BUFFERS=nn

where nn is the number of buffers to use.

The third command is not available on all versions of DOS, and the command format also varies from version to version, so you need to check your DOS manual for this one. It is FASTOPEN. The action of this is to hold the data on the files in the current directory or directories in memory, so that it is not necessary to read it from disk for each file access. This can greatly speed up file handling. Again, there is a trade-off between the number of FASTOPEN entries you allow, and the amount of free memory left for applications.

AUTOEXEC.BAT

The AUTOEXEC.BAT file is an ordinary batch file, and can contain any batch file commands. The only thing special about it is that it runs automatically immediately after CONFIG.SYS. It can be used to set things up as you want them, but of course, these settings can be changed subsequently, at the DOS prompt or in other batch files. AUTOEXEC.BAT can even be used to launch an application immediately on start up.

Among the useful things you can do in the AUTO-EXEC.BAT file is to set initial search paths for files, using the PATH and APPEND commands. These are described in the next chapter.

Normally, when DOS starts, you will be prompted to enter the date and time to set the system clock. If either CONFIG.SYS or AUTOEXEC.BAT is found, these prompts will not appear. If your computer has a real-time clock, this will not be a problem. If it does not, you can include the commands DATE and TIME in AUTOEXEC. BAT, to enable you to make the settings.

Chapter 3

HARD DISK FILE MANAGEMENT

On a hard disk it is easy to generate a large number of files very quickly. Indeed, the whole point of a hard disk is to have all the files you are likely to need quickly to hand. As an example of this, the hard disk on the computer being used to write this book has 1009 files on it, occupying nearly 15mb, and this file will make 1010 when saved very shortly. This particular computer is used primarily for word processing. Many users will generate many more files than this.

Obviously, with this number of files it is far from easy to remember the filenames given to all of them, and also, on seeing a list of all the filenames, to remember what exactly each file is. The limit of eight characters in a filename plus a three character extension (which is not always chosen by the user) does not allow for fully descriptive filenames.

If all the files were simply stored in one directory on the disk, so that giving the DIR command caused all the filenames to be displayed, it would be very difficult to find a particular file in the listing. Even more difficult would be searching through the listing for a particular file when you couldn't quite remember what name you gave it, something which happens to all of us sooner or later.

Hierarchical Filing System

To help with these problems, the operating system supports a hierarchical system of directories and subdirectories. This can be used on floppy disks as well as hard, but is not really necessary with the limited capacity of floppy disks, and few people use the facility. On a hard disk, it is absolutely essential.

The system consists of a root directory, the primary directory on the disk, and a series of subdirectories below this. Both the root directory and the subdirectories can contain any combination of both files and further

37

subdirectories. Subdirectories are not a physical dividing up of the disk in the way that partitions are. Files from different subdirectories can be mixed together on the disk in any order. In fact, files do not even necessarily occupy contiguous areas of the disk.

Normally, one subdirectory will be created when you put DOS on the hard disk. This subdirectory contains the DOS utilities, like the FORMAT, BACKUP, and RESTORE programs, and all the other external commands provided with the operating system. Exactly what this directory contains will depend on the version of the operating system you have.

Subdirectories are given names just like filenames. You can give a subdirectory name an extension, but it is not usual to do so. On a directory listing, subdirectories are indicated by having <DIR> where the file size is normally displayed.

The terms "directory" and "subdirectory" are normally used as follows. The root directory is always called a directory and never a subdirectory. When you are at root level all other directories are referred to as subdirectories. When you make one of these subdirectories the current directory, you can refer to it as a directory or a subdirectory. All the directories below it are subdirectories, and the directory immediately above it is the "parent directory". It is not usual, however, to refer to the root directory as a parent directory. The hierarchical directory structure is shown diagrammatically in Figure 3.1.

The Root Directory
The root directory is the main directory on the disk. When you start DOS from the hard disk, you will normally be placed in the root directory (the only way this will not happen is if you include a command to switch directories in the AUTOEXEC.BAT file).

In general, it is a good idea to keep the root directory as free from clutter as possible. Certain files do have to go in this directory. These include the system files IO.SYS and MSDOS.SYS (IBMBIOS.SYS and IBMBDOS.SYS on PC-DOS, DRBIOS.SYS and DRBDOS.SYS on DRDOS).

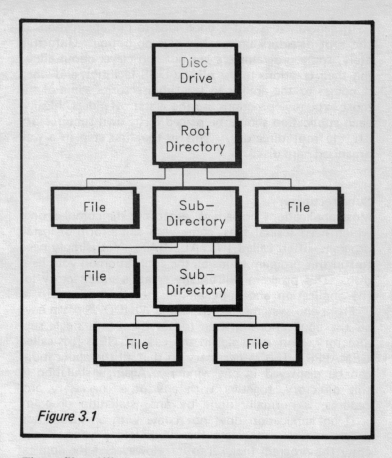

Figure 3.1

These files will not normally appear on directory listings as they are hidden files. This is done to try to prevent accidental deletion or overwriting. The batch files CONFIG.SYS and AUTOEXEC.BAT must also be here. Some application files also insist on being in the root directory if they are to execute properly. The worst even insist on having their data files here.

You may also want to put some utility programs in the root directory, programs such as text editors and screen dumps. However, a better place for these may be in the directory with the DOS utilities, or in a special utilities subdirectory.

In general, it is not a good idea to put applications in the root directory unless they give no option. Unfortunately, some programmers are not too clever about allowing their creations to use all the DOS facilities, and when it comes to the ability to use subdirectories some of the most expensive programs are the worst offenders. Ideally, each application should be placed in its own subdirectory off the root directory. This is the first step in a well organised hard disk.

Subdirectories

Most applications nowadays, especially the complex ones which need several files, come with some form of install program, often called INSTALL.BAT. You simply need to run this program to install the application on your hard disk. This program will usually create a subdirectory for the application and copy all the necessary files into it.

Front-end systems like GEM and WINDOWS often have all the applications written to use them in a single subdirectory. For example, in the case of GEM it is called GEMAPPS. This is necessary so that all the applications can be displayed in one window. Again, installation in this directory, together with any other necessary procedures, is normally done by an installation program.

If an application does not come with an installation program, you can create the subdirectory yourself and copy the program file(s) into it. However, if the application does not recognise subdirectories, you may have problems using the program. It will probably run from within the subdirectory, but may have difficulty loading or saving data files. It may refuse to do so completely, or may insist on always loading and saving from and to the root directory. In other cases, files may be loaded correctly from any subdirectory specified, but when saving a modified file, it may always be sent either to the root directory, or to the subdirectory containing the application, so that you have both the old and new versions. This can be a severe nuisance if you are not aware that it is happening.

The program manual will normally tell you if there are any restrictions on use of this sort. However, many of the examples of this sort of thing are public domain programs which do not come with any sort of manual worthy of the name.

When possible, it is also a good idea to divide the data files used by the program into types, and put each type into its own subdirectory. As an example of this, I use a separate subdirectory for each book. This has advantages when it comes to naming files. With a limit of eight characters, it is hard to create an understandable name which identifies both the book the file belongs to, and which part of the book it is. If you give the subdirectory a name derived from the name of the book, each file within it can be given a simple name like PREFACE.DOC, CH1.MS, INDEX.DOC, and so on.

This is also useful with correspondence. If you use a separate directory for each correspondent, you can save each letter with a filename derived from the date. As, in business, correspondence is always referred to by date, this makes it quick and easy to locate a required letter.

Here again, some programs are unhelpful. They may happily run from a subdirectory, and load and save files from and to that subdirectory, but they may not allow lower levels of subdirectories to be used. Others may insist that all their data files are contained in a single subdirectory, which may be created when the program is installed. There is little that can be done about this sort of thing.

Normally, three levels of subdirectory like this, that is, root directory, one level for application files and one level for data files, is all most people will need to use. A fourth level is commonly used with windowing systems like GEM and WINDOWS (root directory, system level, application level, data level, though not necessarily in that order). In fact, DOS does not set an absolute limit to the number of levels which can be used, but there is an effective limit set by the fact that the complete filename, including all levels of subdirectories, the separating backslashes, and the filename and extension, but not the drive identifying letter and colon, must not exceed 63 characters.

Creating and Using Subdirectories

MKDIR
Subdirectories are created with the command MKDIR. This is followed by the name for the directory you wish to create. The name must conform to the usual DOS rules for allowable characters, and has a maximum length of eight characters. The optional three character extension can be used, but it is not usual to do so with directory names.

Creating a directory in this way, just giving the name, will create a subdirectory off the current directory. You can also create a subdirectory anywhere else on the disk by giving the full path to the subdirectory. For example, if you want to create a new subdirectory off the root called MW, and a subdirectory off this called LETTERS, you could do this with the following commands from the root directory.

```
mkdir mw
mkdir mw\letters
```

Note the use of the backslash "\". This is always used as a separator between directory names in paths. If you were anywhere else but in the root directory, you could create the same directories with the following commands.

```
mkdir c:\mw
mkdir c:\mw\letters
```

In fact, it is not necessary to give the drive identifying letter and colon, (unless another drive is current), because starting a path with the backslash is regarded as a short-hand for the root directory. MKDIR can also be shortened to MD, so the commands above could be reduced to

```
md \mw
md \mw\letters
```

42

CHDIR

The command to change to a directory, that is, to make another directory the current directory, is CHDIR, which can be abbreviated to CD. Following on the above examples, to make MW the current directory from the root directory, you would enter

chdir mw

or just

cd mw

To make mw\letters the current directory, you would enter (from the root directory)

cw mw\letters

If you were in the directory c:\utils and you wanted to change to c:\mw\letters you could use

cd \mw\letters

Finally if you had drive A as the current drive and you were in the directory A:\BASIC you could make a directory c:\qb45\examples current with the command

cd c:\qb45\examples

followed by

c:

to change to drive C. You can change the current directory on a drive other than the current one, but CHDIR will not change the current drive itself. A current directory is maintained for each valid drive, so on making drive A current again with

a:

you would find yourself in the directory A:\BASIC, not in the root directory. This could cause an error if you have changed the disk in drive A in the meantime. You should always make the root directory of a floppy disk drive the current directory before changing disks.

There are some other points which should be noted. The backslash on its own is always a shorthand for the root directory on the current drive, so you can change to the root directory from anywhere with

        cd\

To move back up through the directory structure one step at a time, you can use

        cd . .

For example, if you were in c:\mw\letters and you gave this command, c:\mw would become the current directory, and if you gave it again, the root directory would become current.

RMDIR
Directories which are no longer needed can be removed with the command RMDIR, or RD for short, followed by the directory name. However, you cannot remove a directory which has any files in it. To remove a directory containing files, you should first make it the current directory, and use the command DIR to see if it contains files. You will always see entries for "." and " . . ", as these are markers placed by the operating system when first creating the directory. They do not count as files. If you see any other files, they must be deleted.

This includes any lower levels of subdirectories, even if they are empty. To remove a complex "branch" of subdirectories, you must start at the lowest level, and "prune" your way back up, one level at a time, to the point required.

You cannot delete a directory while it is the current directory, so you would next have to give the command "cd .. ", to move up one level. You should then be able to remove the directory.

If a subdirectory shows no files within it, but you still cannot delete it, it may be that it contains a hidden file. These are created by some applications as part of the paranoid copy protection schemes with which we are plagued. If you need to remove a protected program from a hard disk, check whether it is provided with an "uninstall" or "offhard" utility to do this for you.

The TREE Command

The subdirectory structure of a hard disk, either the whole or selected parts, can be inspected with the TREE command. If given on its own, the command will display the current directory name, and all subdirectories off this. Alternatively, you can give the path specification to the directory where you wish to begin, at either a higher or a lower level. The following example is what was displayed in response to the command

TREE C:\GEMAPPS

on my own computer.

bytes	files	path
524,715	15	c:\gemapps
1,109	1	c:\gemapps\1st_word
63,509	22	c:\gemapps\1st_word\docs
7,046	12	c:\gemapps\1st_word\printers
112,401	9	c:\gemapps\1st_word\tools
1,058,428	148	c:\gemapps\fonts
1,921	5	c:\gemapps\formats
356,415	19	c:\gemapps\gemsys
5,376	2	c:\gemapps\patterns
1,500,512	226	c:\gemapps\store
total files	459	total bytes 3,631,432

Note that individual files are not displayed, only the directory names. However, the number of files and size in bytes of each subdirectory is shown.

Some versions of TREE take a /G switch, which gives a graphical display. Figure 3.2 is an example of this.

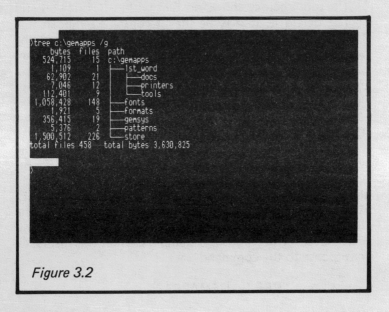

```
)tree c:\gemapps /g
      bytes  files  path
    524,715    15   c:\gemapps
      1,109     1   ├───1st_word
     62,902    21   ├───docs
      7,046    12   ├───printers
    112,401     9   └───tools
  1,058,428   148   ├─fonts
      1,921     5   ├─formats
    356,415    19   ├─gensys
      5,376     2   ├─patterns
  1,500,512   226   └─store
total files 458    total bytes 3,630,825

)
```

Figure 3.2

Floating Drives

A problem with deep levels of subdirectories is the long path names which may need to be typed in commands. If, for example, you were working with two directories, a:\basic and c:\qb45\examples, it would be irritating to have to keep typing these to switch between the two.

This problem can be overcome with the use of "floating drive" identifiers. You can use the command SUBST to substitute a single drive identifier for the long pathnames, and thereafter switch from path to path as simply as from drive to drive.

In order to do this, you need to have drive letters available. This is done with the command LASTDRIVE, which is used in the CONFIG.SYS file. It is a good idea to have at least two extra drive letters available for use with SUBST. For example, if you have a typical single-floppy, single hard disk machine with no RAM disk, drive identifiers A and B will be used for the floppy drive,

46

and the hard disk will be drive C. If you put the line

LASTDRIVE=E

in CONFIG.SYS, this will allow you to use D and E as floating drives.

You could then use the commands

SUBST D: A:\BASIC
SUBST E: C:\QB45\EXAMPLES

and subsequently make these directories current with D: and E:.

You can display the current assignments by entering SUBST without parameters. The assignment for a floating drive can be deleted using the /D option switch, e.g.

SUBST D: /D

You should not use any commands which work on whole disks while any substitutions are in effect. These commands include BACKUP, RESTORE, DISKCOPY, FORMAT, LABEL.

The default LASTDRIVE setting in DOS is supposed to be E:, but this is not to be relied upon. If you want to use floating drives, I would recommend making an explicit setting in CONFIG.SYS.

Running Applications in Subdirectories

In order to run a program in a subdirectory, you normally need to make that directory current, and then give the command to run the program. These two steps can be automated by placing a batch file in the root directory containing the necessary commands. You can then change to the directory and run the program simply by invoking the batch file. You can also include a command in the batch file to change back to the root directory when you exit the application.

An example of such a simple batch file, to launch a program called MYWORD in a directory called MW is as follows:—

    CHDIR MW
    MYWORD
    CHDIR\

Using CHDIR\ (or cd\) from anywhere in the directory structure will always take you back to the root directory. This is useful in a batch file like this, because you may have moved deeper into the directory structure whilst using the program. If, for example, you load a file from a level deeper than the one the program is in, some programs will make the directory from which you are loading the file the current directory. Should you change the current drive whilst using the program, however, this command would take you to the root directory on *that* drive. This command will not cause an error if you are already in the root directory.

Batch files can be much more complex than this, and can do such things as passing information to the application being launched, and automatically backing up files which have been modified when the application is exited. Advanced batch files are covered in Chapter 5.

The ideal root directory, therefore, would contain only the files necessary to the operating system (system and batch files), the subdirectory containing the operating system utilities, subdirectories containing the major applications, and the batch files to launch them. With applications and their data files grouped in their own subdirectories, it should be quick and easy to locate any required file.

The PATH Command
With small utilities, including both those supplied with the operating system and any you may add, it is desirable to have them available from wherever you are in the directory structure, but without having to enter the full path as well as the filename. To enable this, DOS includes the PATH command. This command can be given at any time, and it tells the operating system where to look for command

files. PATH is most commonly used in the AUTOEXEC. BAT file, when DOS is first loaded. Note that PATH only applies to command and batch files, that is, files with the extensions .COM, .EXE, or .BAT. It does not apply to data files.

Normally, when you type a filename at the DOS prompt to run the file as a command, only the current directory is searched for the file. If the file is not in that directory, a FILE NOT FOUND message is displayed. By using PATH, you can list other directories to be searched, giving the full path to each one. Suppose, for example, that you have some utilities in the root directory, some in the MSDOS subdirectory, and some in a directory called UTILS. To make DOS search all of these you would list all the paths to these.

```
C:\
C:\MSDOS
C:\UTILS
```

In the PATH command, the individual paths are separated by semicolons, like this:—

```
PATH C:\;C:\MSDOS;C:\UTILS
```

The operating system only searches the final subdirectory in each path, so that if for instance, you had made UTILS a subdirectory of MSDOS (C:\MSDOS\UTILS), you would still need both paths in the command, like this:—

```
PATH C:\;C:\MSDOS;C:\MSDOS\UTILS
```

You can specify more than one disk drive in the PATH command if required. For example, if you have UTILS directories on both drive C and drive D (it is quite legal to use the same subdirectory name on two or more drives, even if they are logical drives on the same physical disk), the path command would become this:—

```
PATH   C:\;C:\MSDOS;C:\UTILS;D:\UTILS
```

Note in this example that the root directory of drive D would not be searched, though it would if it happened to be the current directory. The current directory is always searched first, followed by the directories listed in the path command, in the order they are listed, unless or until the file is found.

It is possible to use the PATH command to set paths to all the subdirectories where your applications are stored. If this is done, it means that any application can be launched from anywhere within the directory structure simply by typing its name. However, this causes far more problems than it solves. For a start, it involves a very long PATH command, and all the directories listed in that command will be searched in order until the required program file is found. That can drastically slow down the launch of programs well into the PATH list. Secondly, the program will be started without the directory containing it being made the current directory. Some programs do not allow this, and it may also cause difficulties with loading files.

On the whole, the method of using batch files is to be preferred for applications. Remember that the PATH command can be used for batch files, so if you have batch files in the root directory to launch your major applications, and a path command including the root directory, you can still launch those applications wherever you are in the directory structure. Further, you can, by this method, ensure that the application subdirectory is made current before starting the program. To do this, however, you must give the full path to the subdirectory in the batch file, i.e. CD C:\WP, not just CD WP. The current path can be displayed by typing just PATH. It is also a good idea to include the command to make the drive holding the application the current drive, in case another drive is current when you invoke the batch file.

Within batch files, it is possible to add bits to the existing path, and also to save an existing path, substitute a new one, and then revert to the old one later in the batch file. These techniques are sometimes used in the batch files used to start front end systems like some versions of GEM, which may have specific path requirements.

These advanced techniques are covered in Chapter 5.

The APPEND Command

The PATH command cannot be used to enable applications to find data files within the directory structure. By default, only the current directory is searched for data files. If they are anywhere else, you either have to specify the full path to them, or make the subdirectory containing them the current directory.

To enable other specified directories to be searched, the APPEND command is provided. This works much like PATH, but is for data files only. Note that APPEND is used by applications rather than by the operating system, and not all applications are written to use it.

Whereas PATH is normally used only once in a working session, usually in the AUTOEXEC.BAT file, if APPEND is used it is likely to be invoked several times, perhaps once for each application which is launched (providing of course that the application can use it). As an example, suppose you have a database called MYBASE in a directory called MD, and you have two subdirectories off this called CLIENTS and SUPLIERS. In order to allow both of these directories to be searched, the APPEND command would be:—

    APPEND C:\MD\CLIENTS;C:\MD\SUPLIERS

This command could be included in the batch file used to launch the application. The path set by APPEND can be cancelled by entering

    APPEND ;

As the path remains in effect until changed or cancelled, it is a good idea to cancel it (in the batch file, perhaps), as otherwise it would still be used inappropriately by other applications launched subsequently, slowing down operations. An example of such a batch file follows.

    CD C:\MD
    APPEND C:\MD\CLIENTS;C:\MD\SUPLIERS

MYDATA
APPEND :
CD\

APPEND is generally not as useful as PATH, and some operators never use it. In particular, it is not appropriate to programs running under systems such as GEM and WINDOWS, which use icon and menu systems to enable data files to be located and loaded.

One problem with APPEND is that some applications do not use it correctly. They may use it to find files in any specified subdirectory, but may always save modified files to the root directory or the application subdirectory, so that you have two copies of the file, old and new.

Disk Management

A big advantage to having a hard disk is the speed with which files can be located and loaded. With certain applications, such as desk top publishing and some types of CAD program, a hard disk is essential because of the large numbers of file accesses these programs make. The performance of a hard disk, however, can deteriorate over a period of time, because of the way DOS uses the space on the disk.

When first formatted and installed with applications, all the files on the disk will be in one area, and all the files will be in one piece, that is, occupying consecutive sectors on the disk. As the disk is used, however, some files will be deleted. Others, as a result of work done on them, will become longer and will not fit in the space they originally occupied. When this happens, the file will be written to a new area on the disk, and the original file deleted.

This process causes numbers of gaps to be created in the used part of the disk. In order to avoid wasting this space, DOS will save files into these gaps. If DOS starts saving into such a gap, and it is not big enough to take the complete file, the remainder of the file will be placed either in another gap, or in the unused area of the disk. It is this fragmentation of files that causes deterioration of disk performance.

When loading a fragmented file, the operating system reads the first chunk, and then has to go to the file allocation table to find where on the disk the next chunk is placed. If the file is in more than two fragments, this has to be repeated for each fragment. The FAT and the file fragments are likely to be on different tracks, and so a lot of head-stepping from track to track is necessary, and this stepping is the slowest part of hard disk operation. It can be clearly heard as a series of ticking sounds as the head is moved during file loading.

There are ways of minimising file fragmentation, but it cannot be prevented completely. It is not a good idea to delete obsolete files on an ad hoc basis. This creates small gaps and is just inviting fragmentation. It is better to leave old files in place, perhaps renaming them with an extension like .OBS or .OLD, and then to delete a lot in one go. There are utilities which can help with this, particularly in suites of programs like PC Tools De Luxe and Norton Utilities. DRDOS comes with a utility called XDEL which is very useful for deleting files in batches.

This will not completely prevent gaps developing, as the operating system itself deletes some files without the user being aware this is happening. Whenever a file grows in size and is saved, it is quite likely to be saved in full as a new file, and the original then deleted. Many applications also create temporary files during operation which are deleted when the program is terminated. All these lead to gaps.

Fortunately, the process of file fragmentation is a curable one, and there are two main ways of doing this. The first and simplest way is to use a disk compaction program. These are to be found in the suites of disk utilities programs like PC Tools and Norton Utilities already mentioned.

The first step before using such a program is to have a good clear-out of old and unwanted files so that after compaction as much disk space as possible is freed up. The second step is to make a full backup of the hard disk in case anything should go wrong. It is a good idea to have two copies of the backup disks or tape.

The backup programs will often report on the degree to

which file fragmentation has occurred, and will suggest whether or not compaction is advisable. Generally, when using such a program, you should not have resident utility programs, that is, "pop up" programs such as Sidekick or screen dump programs, resident in memory. This can cause the disk to become corrupted. You should not attempt to run such a program from a front-end system like GEM or WINDOWS.

The compaction programs work by shuffling the files around between the used and unused parts of the disk, using a great deal of memory in the process, until all the files are arranged in contiguous sectors. These programs will often, if required, sort files within subdirectories into order (usually alphabetical), which can make it easier to find particular files on directory listings. After a compaction program has been used, disk operations should become noticeably faster, and the arranging of the disk into distinct used and unused parts will ensure that the maximum amount of free space is made available.

If you do not have a compaction utility, the same effect can be achieved by using the BACKUP and RESTORE utilities provided with the operating system. As with compaction, the first step should be to delete all unwanted files. A full backup should then be done. In this case, it is *essential* to make a second copy of the backup disks or tape, as the next step is to format the hard disk. This is necessary because, if it is not done, during the RESTORE process, some restore programs will just put the files back in their original positions.

RESTORE is then used to load the files back onto the hard disk. Note that it is not necessary to use FORMAT /S to put the system files on the disk when formatting it, as these will have been backed up, and will be restored with the other files. When the files are restored, they will be placed from the start of the disk using consecutive segments, so all fragmentation will be eliminated. In a way, the backup and restore method does a more thorough job than compaction programs, as it arranges all files in each subdirectory together on the disk, which compaction programs do not.

Note that you can only do this with a backup program which saves on a file-by-file basis. Some third-party back-up programs copy the hard disk on a sector-by-sector and track-by-track basis. Obviously, such programs will preserve the fragmentation with the files.

It is a good idea to remove any fragmentation before installing any new major application. This avoids having the main program EXE file fragmented, which can slow down the starting of the application.

Of course, this neat arrangement starts to be disrupted as soon as you start using the disk again, so it is a process that needs to be performed periodically to maintain peak performance. With files which are not altered frequently, however, like the font files for DTP, the improvement in performance is permanent and can be quite substantial.

A further factor which concerns operating speed is the way in which DOS handles subdirectories. Each subdirectory can initially take entries for up to 63 files. If you exceed this number, a second area for a second set of 63 files is created elsewhere on the disk. Any number of subsidiary tables can be created. Obviously, having to consult several directory areas in this way will slow down file location just as fragmentation slows loading. Whenever it is possible, it is better to keep the number of files in a single subdirectory to 63 or less.

Chapter 4

SECURITY AND BACKUP PROCEDURES

An essential part of hard disk use is to make backup or security copies of all files. Hard disk failures can and do occur, and the complete contents of a hard disk can be lost in this way. For some people that could represent months of work. Hard disks are also vulnerable to accidental (or malicious) reformatting. This can be a particular problem with computers which are used by several people, for example in schools and colleges. There is also the possibility of a machine being lost by fire, theft or other cause. In some cases, the data on the hard disk may be worth more than the computer.

Backup Methods
Backup copies can be made on to floppy disks, special tape cassettes, or onto another hard disk. Floppy disks are inexpensive, and require no further equipment other than the floppy disk drive which is fitted in virtually all computers. However, a large number of disks may be needed to make a full backup of a hard disk, and the process is also time-consuming. It is necessary to be in constant attendance to insert new disks when required. An advantage of floppy disks is that it is easy to duplicate them for extra security.

Special tape equipment, known as tape streamers, are fast, and fully automatic once the process is started, so that no constant attendance is required. However, the tape streamer drive is an expensive item, often more than the hard disk drive. The tape cassettes are slightly more expensive than the equivalent storage capacity in floppy disks. Recently, questions have been raised over the reliability of tape streamers. It has been suggested that they are less reliable than the hard disks they back up. If correct, this would obviously be a severe drawback. Duplication of backup tapes is not straightforward. It is normally easier to perform the backup twice. This is not possible, of course, if you have lost the hard disk contents and want a security copy of the tape before attempting to restore.

Variants on tape streamers proper include a system for backing up on to video cassettes, and another which uses digital audio tape (DAT) cassettes. The first of these has not found a wide market. The second is very new, and it is too soon to say whether it will succeed. Both claim a price advantage over true tape streamers, but these are now falling in price anyway.

Backing up onto a second hard disk is an interesting possibility. Clearly, it would be fast, and hard disks are reliable (despite what you may read elsewhere) provided they are used correctly. However, if the two drives are mounted in the same machine, it is hardly a backup at all, as if for example, the machine were stolen or destroyed by fire, both copies would be lost. If the backup is made onto a separate and portable hard disk, the method becomes expensive, as hard disks robust enough to be moved regularly are not cheap. Using an unsuitable drive in this way would not be good security practice.

It is backing up onto floppy disks which is the most popular method with individual users, with tape streamers being used mostly in commercial environments, especially with multi-user systems. Backing up onto floppy disks will be described here.

Backup Programs
Hard disks are backed up using a program normally called BACKUP. This stores the files in a special format, so that they can only be put back onto the hard disk with a program provided for this purpose, and normally called RESTORE. The backup program allows files to be split across two disks if necessary, thus minimising the number of disks required. Files from backup format disks cannot be used directly by DOS, but it is possible to make security copies of backup disks with the DISKCOPY utility. There are utility programs available which will convert backup format files so that they can be used by DOS (often to be found in PD and Shareware catalogues).

58

Whether using these have any advantages over using the supplied RESTORE program is another matter.

All current versions of DOS are provided with some form of backup program. These differ in detail, but the facilities offered and the method of use are much the same in all of them. An important point to bear in mind is that there is no single standard backup format clearly established. There are examples of backup programs which can be used with versions of RESTORE from other operating systems (for example the DRDOS backup uses the IBM format), but in general any version of BACKUP must be used with its own RESTORE program.

A further point is that these programs will normally only work with one version of the operating system. If you need to restore onto a machine which normally uses a different version of DOS, you may need to temporarily boot up the version used to make the backup in order to use RESTORE. It is a good idea to keep a suitable system disk with your backup disks. This is not an insignificant point. Complete machine failure is probably just as common as a hard disk failure, so you may well need to be able to switch to another machine to continue work.

There are also independent backup programs available, either as individual products or as part of suites like PC Tools or Norton Utilities. Various advantages are claimed for these, like greater speed or the use of fewer disks. Some of them do store files in a form which can be directly used by DOS, but this is likely to need more storage disks. Personally, I have always used the programs supplied with DOS, and have not found them seriously wanting. One significant virtue of some of the independent programs is that they will work with any version of the operating system, which can make it easier to restore files on to a machine other than the one they were saved from.

Most backup programs store files on a file-by-file basis, and in general it is possible with these to restore selected files, as well as the complete contents of the hard disk. Some of the third party backup programs use a different method, where the entire contents of the disk is stored on a track-by-track and sector-by-sector basis. With these, it may not be possible to restore only part of the saved data.

You do not always have to backup the entire contents of the hard disk. You can give a file specification in the backup command which will enable individual files, files in selected directories, or files with a particular extension to be backed up. Here again, however, some third-party backup programs will only save the entire contents of the hard disk.

The Archive Attribute
DOS stores a number of "attributes" for each file. One of these is called the archive attribute. This is cleared each time a file is backed up, and set again if the file is modified. The backup program can be set to check this bit, and thus only back up files which have been modified since the previous backup. It is also possible only to back up files which have been modified since a given date or time, using the date stamp on the file.

The Backup Operation
This section describes the backup operation using the DOS BACKUP program. However, much of the information is general to all backup programs.

You must ensure that you have sufficient floppy disks available to take all the files which will be saved. In general, you should allow thirty 360K disks for each 10mb of files on the hard disk. Obviously, if you have higher capacity disks (with the appropriate drive), you will need fewer of them. In general, the disks should be formatted before use. However, the DRDOS backup program, and some independent ones, will automatically format unformatted disks during the backup process. This does, however, considerably increase the time the backup takes.

It is sometimes suggested that the number of disks used, and the time taken, to perform a backup can be reduced by backing up only the data files and not installed applications. You do, after all, have the distribution disks for the applications, and could re-install them. However, this overlooks the point that many applications need a lot of customisation to a particular machine, and that this can take some time.

Certain copy-protected programs may cause problems when backing up. Some may simply not be saved, while others may crash the entire process. In some cases they may seem to back up correctly, but may prove to be unrestorable. You may find that some have to be "uninstalled" before backing up, and replaced afterwards. Personally, I operate a boycott on all such protected programs.

The disks should be blank, or at least not contain any files you wish to retain. Like DISKCOPY, BACKUP will overwrite any data on the disk. Certain third-party backup programs use non-standard disk formats, usually in order to pack more data onto the disks. With these, you should follow the program instructions regarding formatting.

The backup disks should be numbered, and you should be careful to use them in the correct sequence. You will need to insert the disks in the correct order when restoring for the operation to work correctly. It is better to number the disks in advance, rather than as they are used. This is especially true with those third-party backup programs which allow two floppy drives to be used (if you have two), as here it is easy to become confused over which disk is which as you shuffle them in and out of the two drives.

If you should happen to get the disks out of order, check to see whether the backup program has given the disks volume labels. Place the disk in drive A, and give the command VOL. This will display the disk label. In the case of backup disks, this will often include the disk number.

It is best to always make the root directory the current directory before giving the backup command. With many RESTORE programs, you will need to be in the same directory when you restore as you were when you backed up for the operation to work correctly. Some are very fussy, and if you are in a different directory when restoring to the one you were in when backing up, it can be difficult or impossible to specify a path which will enable the RESTORE program to find the required file on the backup disk. The root directory is the one directory which can be guaranteed always to exist. By always backing up from within this directory, you introduce a constant factor which should eliminate this difficulty.

The BACKUP Command
The command to back up the entire contents of hard disk drive C: onto floppy disks in drive A: is:—

BACKUP C:\ A: /S

Note that the source drive is given first, followed by the destination drive. The switch /S specifies that the contents of subdirectories are also to be backed up. Without this, only the current directory will be backed up. This switch must always be used when backing up an entire disk.

To back up the files in a single subdirectory, you specify the path to this directory.

BACKUP C:\MW A:

Note that this will only back up the files in the directory MW, and not files in any subdirectories off this, nor the files in the root directory. If you want to back up files in the subdirectories as well, you simply add the /S switch.

BACKUP C:\MW A: /S

Individual files can be backed up by giving the full path and filename, like this example, which would be the command on my computer to back up the file for this chapter.

BACKUP C:\WP50\GMHD\CH4.MS A:

You can also back up selected groups of files using the ? and * wildcards in the normal way.

BACKUP C:\WP50\GMHD\CH?.MS A:

This will backup all the files for all the chapters in this book, the only problem arising with books which have 10 or more chapters.

BACKUP C:\WP50\GMHD\PREFACE.*

This form is useful if you want to back up associated files which have the same name but difference extensions, perhaps .MS and .DOC.

To only back up files which have the Archive attribute set, you use the /M switch. It is still possible to back up either the whole disk, selected directories, or specified files, but only files which both meet the file specification and have the archive bit set (which generally means that they have been modified since the last backup — /M for modified) will be saved. This includes any new files generated since the last backup.

BACKUP C:\MW\LETTERS A: /M

This will back up any new or modified files in the LETTERS subdirectory since the last backup. It will not backup any files in subdirectories off LETTERS. If you want to do this, you can add the /S switch as well. The switches do not have to be in any particular order.

BACKUP C:\MW\LETTERS A: /M /S

To back up only files which were last changed or created since a given date, you use the /D switch. This is followed by a colon, and then the date. The form in which the date must be given depends on which version of DOS you are using. As examples, in MS-DOS 3.2 it is always given in the form *dd-mm-yy*. In DRDOS, the format is dependent on the COUNTRY command given in the CONFIG.SYS file, and would be *dd-mm-yy* in most European countries, *mm-dd-yy* in the USA, and *yy-mm-dd* in Japan. The following example would back up all files on the hard disk C: modified or created since 1st March 1990, using U.K. date format.

BACKUP C: A: /S /D:01-03-90

DRDOS BACKUP also has the ability to backup only files created or modified after a given time. The switch is /T and the time is given in the format *hh:mm:ss*.

BACKUP C: A: /S /T:14:30:00

This example will back up all files created or modified after half past two in the afternoon.

The /M, /D, and /T (where available) switches can be combined if required.

Normally, the backup program will overwrite files on the backup disk. If you do not want this to happen, for example if you have a number of files in a subdirectory backed up on a disk, and are using the /M switch to update only those files which have been changed, you can use the /A switch. This adds the files to those already on disk, without deleting the existing ones.

BACKUP C:\WP50\GMHD A: /A /M

If you modify a file several times and back it up in this way, all the versions are saved, using modified filename extensions. When you use RESTORE, all are restored in turn, leaving you with the most up-to-date version on the destination disk.

The problem with the /A switch used in this way is that it can fill up the backup disk rather quickly. For a daily backup of work in progress, the XCOPY command, which is described later, can be preferable.

BACKUP Log Files
A final option switch, included on the DRDOS BACKUP, and some others, produces a log of the backup disks which is stored on the source disk. This log is a record of which backup disk each backup file is stored on. Normally, when you want to restore a single file from your backup disks, the RESTORE program will prompt you to insert each disk in turn until it finds it. As the log is a straight text

file, you can inspect it with TYPE, and find the disk
containing the file you require (or the start of it, if it is
split over more than one disk). When asked to insert backup disk 001, you can insert this disk instead. RESTORE
will normally display a message telling you the wrong disk
has been inserted, and asking you if you want to proceed
anyway. If you answer "Y", RESTORE should find and
restore the file.

The log file is particularly useful with backup programs
which concatenate files into a single unit on the backup
disk, so that you cannot find which files are on which
disk using DIR. The IBM and DRDOS backup programs
are of this sort. With MS-DOS BACKUP programs, the
backed up files remain as individual files on disk, so you
can find particular files with DIR.

RESTORE Programs
RESTORE programs are direct counterparts of the BACK-
UP programs they are designed to be used with, and have
similar options. As stated above, in order to restore files
correctly, you need to use the RESTORE program which
matches the BACKUP program used to save the files, and
in many cases you also need to be using the same version
of the operating system used when restoring.

The form of the restore command varies more from
version to version than does the backup command. Therefore, to find the exact syntax required you must consult
your DOS manual. As an example of the variability, the
MS-DOS 3.2 version of RESTORE requires the following
command to restore all the files from drive A: to drive C:

RESTORE A: *.* /S

You would have to be in the root directory of drive C: to
use this command successfully. On DRDOS, the command
to do the same thing would be this:—

RESTORE A: C:\/S

In general, to restore a single file, you must give the full
path and file specification.

RESTORE A: C:\MW\LETTERS\FRED1.DOC

Groups of files can also be restored using wildcards.

RESTORE C:\GEMSYS\GEMAPPS\FONTS\
PAL???RM.ELQ

The option switches provided will also vary, but the following are common examples.

/S restores subdirectories as well as the specified directory.

/P prompts for permission before restoring hidden or read-only files. (You may find this does not work if you have backed up any hidden files created as part of copy-protection schemes.)

/A only restores files which were last modified on the working disk on or after the given date. The date is given in the same form as for the /D switch to BACKUP.

/B only restores files which were last modified on the working disk on or before the given date. The date is given in the same form as for the /D switch to BACKUP.

/N only restores files which no longer exist on the working disk. This is very useful where you know that some files have been deleted, but you do not know which.

/M only restores files which have been modified on the working disk, or which have been deleted, since the back-up was taken. This switch is not found on all RESTORE programs.

If you attempt to restore files from backup disks, and you get the message "No files found to restore", when you know that the files are on the disks (you can use DIR on these disks), the problem may well be the one mentioned earlier, that you are not in the same directory as you were when taking the backup. The answer is to change to that directory if it exists, and if it does not, to create it.

Backup Policy
It is not really good enough to perform backups on an ad hoc basis, as and when you have the time, or when you remember. The intervals between irregular backups tend

to become longer and longer, and a lot of work can be lost if an "incident" occurs. You need to have a fixed, regular backup procedure which gives you security copies of all work all the time.

Obviously, it is not practical to perform a full backup every time the computer is used. Nor is it necessary, as you will normally only modify a few files in a working session, perhaps only one. The purpose of the full backup is to save not only your work files, but also your installed program files, in the form in which you have installed them. Customising programs to your requirements also represents a considerable investment of time.

There is therefore a need for a daily backup of work actually done (more precisely a session backup), and of a periodic, perhaps monthly, backup of the entire disk. It is also a good idea to have an intermediate stage between these two, a selective weekly backup of the subdirectories used in current work. This can help prevent too much data accumulating on the daily backup disks.

The full backups will need to be performed using a backup program, as trying to save the files one by one on to floppies would be wholly impractical. It is best to have two complete sets of backup disks, and to use them alternately. That is, you perform your first backup on set one, the second onto set two, the third onto set one, and so on. In this way, should a failure occur during the actual backup procedure, you will not have lost both your work disk and the backup copy. You should be able to recover everything from the previous full backup, plus the weekly and daily backups.

The weekly backup is also best done using a backup program. You should have a set of disks for each of the subdirectories containing a major application, and the backup should cover both this directory and any subdirectories from it containing data files. In this way, both work files and the application, and any configuration files, are saved. As with the full backup, it is a good idea to have two sets of disks and use them alternately.

The daily backups are a slightly different matter. The daily backup disks will contain work currently in progress.

This is work which is most likely to be needed urgently. If your machine should fail, you need to be able to access this work as quickly and as easily as possible, by using another machine which may have a different operating system version. It is therefore sensible for the files on the day disks to be in DOS format.

The Archive attribute is very useful in daily backups. It enables you only to save the files you have actually been working on, but ensures that all files which have been modified are saved. You could do a daily backup simply using COPY, but you then have to remember all the files you have worked on. If, for example, you have used a spelling checker with a word processor, and added some words to it, it would be easy to forget that the supplementary directory file has been modified.

XCOPY

Most versions of DOS include a program called XCOPY. This copies files in DOS format, and can also (amongst other things) check the archive bit on files, and thus only save files modified since "last time". Like BACKUP, when XCOPY copies a file, it can clear the Archive attribute.

If you launch applications using a batch file, it is also possible to include XCOPY in that file, so that it runs automatically when the application is exited, saving all work done. You can also include a prompt in the batch file to tell you to insert the daily backup disk. Here is an example of such a batch file.

```
@echo off
cd wp50
wp.exe
cls
cd\
echo Current files will be backed up to drive A:
echo Please insert the disk labelled
echo 'WP DAY DISK — DOS FORMAT' in drive A:
echo
echo Press CTRL-C to abort the backup operation.
```

68

```
echo
pause
xcopy c:\wp50 a: /s/m/e
echo Backup completed — you may remove the disk.
```

Should you for any reason not want to perform the
backup (perhaps because you entered the program only to
read a file), pressing CTRL-C when the message appears
allows you to halt the batch process. The pause command
gives you a chance to insert the appropriate disk. It causes
a message "press any key to continue" (or similar) to be
displayed.

The general form of the XCOPY command is similar to
the internal COPY, but it has a number of extra option
switches. In the above example, three are used.

/S causes copies from subdirectories as well the directory given in the source specification to be copied.

/M is the same as in the BACKUP command, and causes
only files which have been modified or created since the
last backup or use of XCOPY to be copied.

/E causes empty subdirectories as well as those containing files (modified/new files if /M is specified) to be
copied. The use of this switch is not essential. It can only
be used in conjunction with /S.

The files and subdirectory structure created on the disk
by XCOPY are pure DOS, so there is no problem about
using the files with other versions of DOS on other computers, or about being in different directories when saving
and recovering the files. Files can be copied from the daily
backup disk on to the working disk with the ordinary DOS
COPY command, though if you want to copy the complete contents of the disk, including the directory structure, onto the working disk, XCOPY allows it to be done
in a single command. If you want to make a complete
copy of the backup disk on to another floppy, for added
security, use DISKCOPY.

Apart from the option switches listed above, XCOPY
has a number of other options.

/A is similar to /M, but does not reset the archive bit
after copying, whereas with /M it is reset.

/D only copies files which have been changed on or after the given date. The date is specified in the same way as for the similar BACKUP option (see previously).

/P asks for confirmation before copying each file.

/V verifies each copy as it is written, to check that it has been copied correctly. Useful if you are unsure of the efficiency of your disk drive.

/W waits until a key is pressed before starting the copying operation. This is to allow you to swap disks before starting the copying. It could have been used instead of the PAUSE in the example batch file above. Copying can be abandoned at this stage with CTRL-C.

The DRDOS version of XCOPY includes some additional options.

/C can be used instead of /P and has the same effect.

/H will include any system files in the source directory in the copy. The default is for them to be left out.

/R will overwrite any read-only files in the destination.

In general, XCOPY will not overwrite files in the destination disk. New files will be added to the existing files. However, if you work on a file over several sessions, backing up at the end of each session, as the file is copied each time it will overwrite the previous version. This helps prevent the daily backup disk from becoming too full.

XCOPY cannot split files across two or more disks. If you are using a program which generates very large files, for instance DTP, so that the files which need to be backed up overflow a single daily backup disk, you will need to use BACKUP rather than XCOPY. Some DTP programs can generate single files larger than 360K if many illustrations are included. If 360K is the largest floppy drive capacity you have, you will need to use BACKUP to make any sort of copy onto floppy disks.

When the weekly backup has been performed successfully, the files on the daily backup disk can be erased. Should the daily disk fill up with data in less than a week, the answer is to perform the "weekly" backup more often. On the other hand, with programs which are only used rarely, the weekly backup may be omitted, so that you only have the full backup and the daily backup disks for the appropriate subdirectories.

Preserving Your Hard Disk Contents

The fear of accidential or malicious reformatting of a hard disk is one which haunts many people. In general, it is hard to avoid, as the program which does it, FORMAT, has to be present on the hard disk to allow formatting of floppies, an operation which most users need to perform fairly frequently.

DRDOS has advantages here. With this operating system, FORMAT is not and indeed cannot be used on hard disks. All hard disk formatting is done with FDISK. It is far from essential to have FDISK present on the hard disk, unless you have two operating systems on a partitioned disk. For most people, when it is needed you are quite likely to have to boot up the operating system from floppies anyway. Leaving FDISK off the hard disk gives a good deal of protection against accidental reformatting, but would not much impede a determined malefactor.

Some measure of protection can be obtained by using a "volume label" on your hard disk. A volume label is a name which can be given to any disk, hard or floppy, using the LABEL command. Where a label has been given, the DOS format command will prompt for that volume name before allowing you to reformat the disk.

This in itself is not much protection, as the volume label is displayed every time you use DIR. However, there is a trick which can be used to give some degree of security. As well as the normal alphanumeric characters which can be included in filenames (and the volume label is a modified filename), it is possible to include the character code 255, which prints as a blank. This can be entered using the numeric keypad and the ALT key. You hold down the ALT key, and then type 255 on the keypad (not the "top row" numeric keys). The character is inserted when you release the ALT key.

If you include this character somewhere in the volume label, it will of course not display as part of the name, but it will be necessary to enter it when FORMAT prompts for the volume label. This therefore gives a reasonable degree

71

of protection.

This protection is not total, since the volume label can be changed at any time with the LABEL command, and you do not need to give the existing label to do this. However, for those who do not know the cause of this problem, they would also not know this simple cure. In DRDOS, you could, of course, apply password protection to the LABEL program.

Chapter 5

ADVANCED USERS SECTION

This chapter contains an assortment of ideas and information for those with a good knowledge of DOS and of computing generally. The information in this section is not essential for the use of a hard disk, but includes things which can save a lot of time and effort for those who are not frightened off by technicalities.

Batch Files
In previous chapters we have seen how batch files can be used to launch programs and to perform automatic daily backups. In fact, any collection of commands which is used frequently can be put into a batch file to save having to type them in full each time. Few users make as much use of batch files as they could. However, it is in starting programs and in things associated with this that batch files can be most valuable, and are perhaps least used.

Passing Parameters
When starting many programs, it is possible to give a "command tail" after the program name. This command tail can include such things as the name of a data file to be loaded automatically when the program starts, and sometimes option switches similar to those used when DOS commands are called.

On the face of it, this facility would seem to be lost when a batch file is used to start a program, but in fact it is not. You can, in effect, give the batch file a command tail, and the items in this command tail can be passed to the program, or used for other purposes.

In the previous chapter an example of a batch file which does an automatic backup was given. This was, in fact, a simplified form of the batch file which I use to launch the word processor which is being used to write this. The full version of this batch file, which uses parameter passing, is given here.

```
@echo off
cd wp50
cd %2
\wp50\wp.exe %1
cls
cd\
echo Current files will be backed up to drive A:
echo Please insert the ^[[33mYellow ^[[32mdisk
          labelled
echo 'WP DAY DISK — DOS FORMAT' in drive A:
echo
echo Press CTRL-C to abort the backup operation.
echo
pause
xcopy c:\wp50 a: /s/m/e
echo Backup completed — you may remove the disk.
```

Note in particular the third and fourth lines. The "%1" and "%2" in these lines are variable names which can be used in batch files. When parameters are given after the batch filename, these are assigned to these variable names in sequence. In this particular case, the first parameter is passed to the program, and in fact would be the name of a file to load on running, and the second is the name of a subdirectory off the directory wp50 (the main application subdirectory), which is made the current directory before running the application.

As an example of the use of this file, to launch the application, loading the file for this chapter and switching to the subdirectory containing it, I would type:—

        wp ch5.ms gmhd

The filename used for the chapter, ch5.ms, is assigned to the variable name%1, and the subdirectory name gmhd is assigned to the variable name %2. This order is used, rather than giving the directory name first followed by the filename, as I am more likely to want to load a file from the wp50 directory, without specifying a subdirectory, than the converse.

74

The strange characters in line 7 are in fact the escape sequences for the ANSI screen driver used on my computer, which make the word "yellow" (I use colour-coded disks) actually appear in yellow, with the following text reverting to the normal green. If you think this is a little over the top, you should see my two-line multicoloured DOS prompt!

File Renaming in Batch Files

A feature of the GEM system is a number of "desktop accessories" which are loaded with the system, and can be called from within any GEM application. These can include a clock, calculator, and a screen capture utility called "Snapshot". When loaded, however, these take up some space in memory, and may make it difficult or impossible to use some memory-intensive GEM applications like DTP programs.

This does cause some problems, as these programs, if present in the GEMSYS subdirectory, are loaded automatically when GEM is started. It is difficult to have them present for some GEM programs, but not for others.

The problem can be avoided by using separate batch files for launching GEM as a system, and for launching the DTP program. Since the accessories are identified by the .ACC extension to their filenames, if this extension is altered by renaming, they will not be found when GEM starts, and will not therefore be loaded.

This in fact gives two options with the DTP program. By launching it from its own batch file, it will load and run with maximum memory available. Alternatively, by running GEM first from its batch file, and then launching the DTP program from the GEM Desktop, the DTP program can be run with the accessories present, provided the computer has enough memory to allow this.

The two batch files to do this are given here. First, the one to launch GEM, and second, the one to launch the DTP program.

```
IF "%OS%"=="CDOS" SUSPEND=ON
IF "%OS%"=="CPCDOS" SUSPEND=ON
```

```
CD \GEMAPPS\GEMSYS
IF EXIST *.ACX REN *.ACX *.ACC
GEMVDI %1 %2 %3
CD\

@echo off
IF "%OS%"=="CDOS" SUSPEND=ON
IF "%OS%"=="CDOS386" SUSPEND=ON
cd \gemapps\gemsys
if exist *.acc ren *.acc *.acx
gemvdi \publish\publish.app
ren \gemapps\gemsys\*.acx *.acc
cd\
```

These files also show how decision making can be used
in batch files. In the fourth line of the first, IF EXIST is
used to determine whether there are any files in the
current directory (which has been made \GEMAPPS\
GEMSYS in line 3) with the extension .ACX. If there are,
they are renamed to the extension .ACC, so that they are
loaded as accessories. This line is included in this batch
file in case the batch file to run the DTP program has,
on a previous occasion, not completed correctly, as could
happen if the DTP program crashed, which it does.

IF EXIST is also used in the second example to detect
if there are any .ACC files present. This is not, in fact,
essential, as if there are no such files, there will simply be
a "File Not Found" message displayed, and the batch file
will continue. The IF test is used purely to keep things
tidy. No test is used when renaming the files back to the
.ACC extension, as there should always be such files
present at this stage. Note that the full file specification,
including the full path, is used here. This is because the
current directory may have been changed during the run
of the DTP program. (For clarity and conciseness, the
automatic backup lines have been removed from these
examples.)

Note that the first file, which is modified from the
batch file provided on the GEM distribution disks, allows
up to three parameters to be passed to GEMVDI. It is not

commonly known that if, for example, you type

GEM PAINT

at the DOS prompt, you can load GEM and automatically start GEM PAINT without having to use the desktop. Further, you could type

GEM PAINT \IMAGES\MYPIC.IMG

and start GEM and the application, and load the image file ready for work on it.

Changing the PATH Setting
As well as specifying a complete new path in a batch file, it is possible to add new paths to the end of the existing setting. This is done by retrieving the existing path, using %PATH%. It is possible either to add bits to the end, or to the beginning, of the existing path, as in these examples.

path %PATH%;c:\basic2;c:\publish

(this adds to the end)

path a:;%PATH%

(this adds to the beginning).

It is also possible to store the existing path, and replace it with a completely new, or modified, one, and restore it later in the batch file. Here is an example of an experimental batch file which will do this.

```
path
set oldpath=%path%
path %path%;c:\temp
path
path %oldpath%
path
```

Figure 5.1 shows this batch file, and the result of executing

77

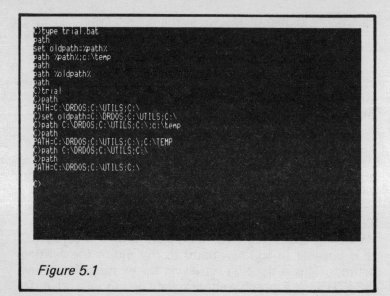

```
C>type trial.bat
path
set oldpath=%path%
path %path%;c:\temp
path
path %oldpath%
path
C>trial
C>path
PATH=C:\DRDOS;C:\UTILS;C:\
C>set oldpath=C:\DRDOS;C:\UTILS;C:\
C>path C:\DRDOS;C:\UTILS;C:\;c:\temp
C>path
PATH=C:\DRDOS;C:\UTILS;C:\;C:\TEMP
C>path C:\DRDOS;C:\UTILS;C:\
C>path
PATH=C:\DRDOS;C:\UTILS;C:\

C>
```

Figure 5.1

it. Note that this can only be done in batch files. It cannot be done from direct (keyboard) commands.

Subdirectories and SUBST

As mentioned in Chapter 3, some programs cannot use subdirectories very well, and this can make file organisation a problem. However, provided such programs allow you to switch drives, it is possible to assign subdirectories to floating drives, and thereby fool the program into using your subdirectories.

One program which is difficult with subdirectories is dBASE III plus, especially when using the "Assistant" menuing system. It does, however, allow easy switching of drives. You could therefore use SUBST to assign subdirectories to drives, and this can be done automatically in a batch file. This could be done either by giving actual directories in the batch file, or by using parameters. The first would be suitable if you only need to use one or two subdirectories, the second being preferable if you have many data file subdirectories.

Here is an example batch file for the first method:—

78

```
CD DBASE
SUBST E:  C:\DBASE\CLIENTS
SUBST F:  C:\DBASE\PERSDAT
DBASE.EXE
SUBST E:  /D
SUBST F:  /D
CLS
CD\
```

Here is an example using parameters:

```
CD DBASE
SUBST E:  %2
SUBST F:  %3
DBASE.EXE  %1
SUBST E:  /D
SUBST F:  /D
CLS
CD\
```

Here, the second and third parameters given after the batch filename are the subdirectories to be substituted. The first parameter is the name of a dBASE program to be run automatically when the application starts. You can, of course, add automatic backup or other features to these files, remembering that any substitutions should be removed *before* using BACKUP, or any other program which works on the whole disk.

The first method is convenient if you only have one or two subdirectories containing your data files. The second is more flexible if you use many subdirectories.

More on IF
The IF command can only be used in batch files. It allows conditional execution of DOS commands, depending on the results of a test. The range of tests which can be used is quite limited, but useful things can be done, as we have seen already.

The first thing you can test for, as we have already seen, is the existence of a file. This file can be anywhere on the disk, or indeed on other disks in any valid drive on the computer, provided you give the path in the filespec. This can include RAM drives. The form of this test is

IF EXIST filespec command

or

IF NOT EXIST filespec command

The second test is whether two strings are identical. Normally one string will be directly included in the command, and the other will be a batch file variable or an environment variable. This command takes the form

IF string1==string2 command

or

IF NOT string1==string2 command

Note that the equals sign is double. The strings should be enclosed in quotation marks to avoid problems if a parameter does not exist.

The third test is for the error level returned by a previous program. Many applications, and some DOS external commands, return an error level, a numerical value which depends on the degree of success of the program. If a command completes successfully with no problems, the error level returned is normally zero. Any difficulties encountered will result in a higher level being returned. The error levels corresponding to various events will be found in applications manuals. You can use these with IF to take appropriate action if specific errors occur.

The test is true if the error level returned is equal to or higher than the number specified in the command. If you want to check for several possible error levels, you must check for the highest first.

This command takes the form

IF ERRORLEVEL number command

or

IF NOT ERROR LEVEL number command

Any DOS command can be executed as the result of an
IF test, but the most useful, in many cases, is the command GOTO. This is another command which can only be
used in batch files, and it is used to branch within the file,
allowing more than one command to be selectively
executed.

Branching in Batch Files
Normally, batch files are executed in the sequence of the
lines. However, this sequence can be altered by using the
GOTO command. This command, which can only be used
within batch files, allows control to be transferred to a
line following a label.

A label is a string of characters. It must be preceded by
a colon, and should be on a line of its own within the
batch file. To jump unconditionally to this label, you use

GOTO label

Note that the label name in the GOTO command should
not be preceded by the colon, nor should it be enclosed in
inverted commas.

Normally, however, GOTO is used in conjunction with
IF.

IF condition GOTO label

or

IF NOT condition GOTO label

The condition can be any of those listed above. GOTO
can be used for forward or backward jumps, so it could be
used to create loops in batch files. This needs care,

however, as you need to make sure that such a loop will terminate. With the limited language of batch files, it is easy to create infinite loops.

Using CHKDSK

CHKDSK is a utility supplied as part of DOS. It should be used regularly to check on the condition of your hard disk.

When used, CHKDSK will check the integrity of your data on the disk, and will report on a number of other things. It can also be used to recover lost space on the disk, and occasionally will recover a corrupted file.

If you just give the command CHKDSK, it will operate on the current disk, and will report on the total disk space, the space used for and the number of directories, the space used by and the number of user files, the available disk space, and the total memory in the computer and the free memory. It will also report any problems it finds on the disk.

If CHKDSK finds any corrupted files or directories on the disk, it will display information about them on the screen. Normally, these are displayed when the program ends, but, by specifying the /V switch (verbose display), they are displayed as the program runs.

CHKDSK C: /V

Additional information may be displayed if the /V switch is used, depending on which version you have.

CHKDSK is mainly intended to report on the condition of a disk (it can in fact be used on hard or floppy disks), but it can also help to recover some types of corrupted files. It can help here in two cases. Firstly, where part of a directory tree has become inaccessible, and secondly, when the file allocation table record (of where parts of a file have been stored) has become corrupted. Both these problems lead to what are known as "lost clusters". CHKDSK finds these lost clusters and can, optionally. convert them into files. To perform this conversion, you must specify the /F (fix) option.

If you do not specify this option switch, lost clusters will be reported, but not converted.

It is not possible for CHKDSK to tell which lost clusters belong to which file, so it converts each group of clusters into a separate file, and it names these FILEnnnn.CHK, where nnnn represents a number, allocated in series. The first recovered file is therefore FILE0001.CHK, the second FILE0002.CHK, and so on. It is unusual for there to be a larger number of them.

It is then possible to examine the contents of these recovered files. If they are text files, this is relatively easy, and, if they are parts of a damaged file, it may be possible to rebuild it with a text editor or word processor. With more complex file types, such as from databases, files may also be recoverable, though with more effort, and you may need to be familiar with the file structure. If the files contain executable code, recovery may be impossible or unwise.

Often, files recovered in this way will prove to be old, deleted versions of files, or temporary files which have been created and deleted by applications. In these cases, the files can be deleted and the space recovered for re-use.

If you attempt to load a data file into an application, and only part of it loads, or the application reports it as corrupt, it is worth using CHKDSK to see if any corruption has occurred, and can be corrected. It is also worth using CHKDSK regularly, perhaps once a week, to check for and recover any clusters which have become lost when deleting files.

You can also use CHKDSK to check on individual files. It will tell you whether the file is in one contiguous block, or whether it is fragmented. Figure 5.2 shows the result of using CHKDSK in this way.

This information is displayed after the normal information about the amount of disk space used and memory, etc. The exact wording of the message may vary from version to version.

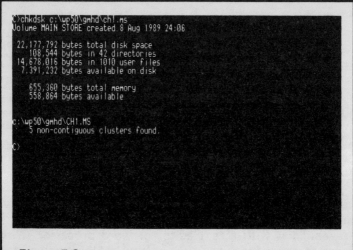

```
C:\>chkdsk c:\wp50\gmhd\ch1.ms
Volume MAIN STORE created 8 Aug 1989 24:06

 22,177,792 bytes total disk space
    108,544 bytes in 42 directories
 14,678,016 bytes in 1010 user files
  7,391,232 bytes available on disk

    655,360 bytes total memory
    558,864 bytes available


c:\wp50\gmhd\CH1.MS
    5 non-contiguous clusters found.

C:\>
```

Figure 5.2

Depending on which version of DOS you have, CHKDSK may have additional option switches, as in the following list. Some of these are exclusive to DRDOS.

/A — Normally, when used, CHKDSK will display the amount of available memory on the machine, and the amount of free memory. Using this switch displays this information only.

/B — This switch causes CHKDSK to search all the files on a disk, to locate and mark any bad blocks. If none is found, nothing will be displayed. This option considerably increases the time CHKDSK takes to execute.

/C — This causes all the cluster numbers of the bad files to be displayed.

/D — This locates the directories on the disk so that in the event of corruption you can attempt to recover files and directories with a suitable disk editor, such as the one in PC TOOLS. Considerable knowledge of disk structure and storage is needed to do this.

/L — When you specify this switch, CHKDSK will attempt to rebuild a corrupted File Allocation Table. You must zero any corrupted areas on the disk before this

84

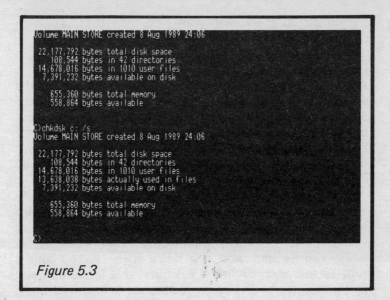

```
Volume MAIN STORE created 8 Aug 1989 24:06

22,177,792 bytes total disk space
   108,544 bytes in 42 directories
14,678,016 bytes in 1010 user files
 7,391,232 bytes available on disk

   655,360 bytes total memory
   558,864 bytes available

C)chkdsk c: /s
Volume MAIN STORE created 8 Aug 1989 24:06

22,177,792 bytes total disk space
   108,544 bytes in 42 directories
14,678,016 bytes in 1010 user files
13,638,038 bytes actually used in files
 7,391,232 bytes available on disk

   655,360 bytes total memory
   558,864 bytes available

C)
```

Figure 5.3

option can be used.

/M — This option checks for any bad blocks, and gives you the option of mapping any new bad blocks. This operation greatly increases the time CHKDSK takes to execute.

/P — This option displays the parent blocks for all directories.

/R — This option will attempt to recover any lost directories which were contained in the root directory. Before using this, you must delete any corrupted files in the root directory.

/S — Shows the actual file space. Space is allocated in (normally) 512 byte sectors. The normal display of space occupied by user files is the full total of all occupied sectors. However, most files will not completely fill the last sector they occupy. This option displays the amount of disk space *actually containing data.* If you have a large number of small files, it may be very much less than the total space occupied. This information is perhaps more interesting than useful. Figure 5.3 shows the display with and without the use of this switch.

You should check with your DOS manual to see which of these options are available to you.

Data Allocation and Files
All disks are divided into sectors, and a sector is the smallest amount of data which can be read from or written to a disk. To modify a single byte, a complete sector must be read in, modified in memory, and then written out again. Normally, sectors are 512 bytes in size (on both hard and floppy disks), but early Apricot computers used a hard-disk sector size of 1024 bytes (1K).

Each sector has a number which DOS uses to identify it. This number is stored as a 16-bit unsigned binary number, which means it can have one of 65536 different values (64K). This sets a limit on the number of sectors which can be addressed as a single drive. As the limit is 64K sectors each of half a kilobyte, this limits disk size to the 32 megabytes already mentioned (a megabyte being 1K kilobytes). Hard disks larger than 32mb have to be partitioned into smaller logical drives, each of which must be less than this limit.

On DOS 4.0 and higher, and DRDOS, this limit has been raised to 512mb per petition by extending the size of the number to 20 bits.

Although the sector is the smallest unit of storage which can be used, files are normally assigned space in "clusters". A cluster can be one or more sectors. On a floppy disk, clusters are normally two sectors. On the 10mb hard disk fitted to early IBM PC XT computers, the cluster size was 8 sectors. Later, this was felt to be excessive, causing too much space to be wasted. Nearly all hard disks now assign space in clusters of four sectors. This means that the smallest space which any file can occupy is two kilobytes.

It follows from this that you should try to avoid creating too many very small files. These will use up disk space much faster than you might expect.

On the one hand, you should avoid creating large numbers of not very useful batch files. Even if not very big in terms of bytes, they still take up at least 2K each.

On the other hand, there is no point in trying to keep batch files as small as possible. You can include extra commands, or remarks to remind you what the file does, and how, without using up any more disk space. However, if you go just one byte over the 2K, your file will occupy 4K!

DOS Disk Structure

DOS divides a disk into two parts, a small system area which it uses itself, and a much larger data area, where user data is stored. The system area is itself subdivided into three distinct sections, which are called the boot sector, the File Allocation Table (FAT), and the root directory.

The boot sector is the very first sector on the disk. It holds a very short "bootstrap" program which begins the process of loading DOS into the computer. This sector is in fact found on all DOS disks, hard and floppy, even if they do not carry the other system files. The boot "sector" is exactly that, a single sector of 512 bytes.

The FAT is used to record the status of each part of the disk. It contains a record for every cluster (not sector) on the disk. The records are in the form of a table of numbers. If the number for a cluster is zero, it indicates that it is free for use. Any other number indicates that the cluster is occupied. The actual number recorded is used to keep track of which clusters belong to which file.

The directory entry for each file contains the number of the first cluster belonging to that file. If the file contains more than one cluster, the FAT entry for the first cluster will contain the number of the second cluster, the FAT entry for the second will contain the number for the third, and so on to the last cluster for the file. The last cluster contains a special code indicating that it is the end of the file. If a file consists of only a single cluster, the FAT entry for that cluster will contain the end-of-file code.

You can see from this that the FAT is a vital part of DOS file management. In fact, it is so important that DOS actually keeps two copies of the FAT on disk. The second copy is never actually used by DOS, but there are third-party utilities which use it to attempt file recovery should the first copy become corrupted.

The root directory is the one directory which is found on every disk. It exists even before any files are recorded onto the disk. This is quite different to subdirectories, which are created only on demand.

The directory entry for each file consists of the filename, the size of the file, the date and time stamp for the file, the file attributes, and the number of the first cluster of the file. The filename can hold up to eight characters, plus a three-character extension, which is optional. The date and time stamps are updated each time a file is saved, but are not altered if the file is opened and read only.

The attributes are a set of eight "flags", which can be either set or clear. The directory attribute is set if the entry is for a subdirectory rather than a file. The hidden and system attributes are used primarily for the DOS system files. These files do not appear on directory listings, and are also invisible to COPY and some other DOS commands. Some copy-protected applications also create hidden files. The read-only attribute protects files from being modified, and the archive attribute records whether a file has been modified since it was last backed up.

The root directory is limited in size. On most hard disks, it has space for 512 entries. This includes both data files and subdirectories off the root. Since it is easy to have many more files than this on a hard disk, this is one reason why you should organise your files into subdirectories.

Subdirectories are stored in the data portion of the disk, and are recorded in the FAT like any other data file. The data in the subdirectory is, however, like that in the root directory, with entries for each file in that directory, and also for further subdirectories off it. Unlike the root directory, a subdirectory is not of a fixed size. It can grow, just like a data file, to be as big as required. Space is, in fact, allocated in sections big enough for 63 file entries. Having a subdirectory in several parts can increase the time taken to find files, however, so there are speed advantages to keeping the number of files in a subdirectory to 63 or less if possible.

Index

? Wildcard	62
* Wildcard	62, 65
/A switch in BACKUP	64
/A switch in CHKDSK	84
/A switch in RESTORE	66
/A switch in XCOPY	69
/B switch in CHKDSK	84
/B switch in RESTORE	66
/C switch in CHKDSK	84
/C switch in XCOPY	70
/D switch in BACKUP	63
/D switch in CHKDSK	84
/D switch in XCOPY	69
/E switch in XCOPY	69
/F switch in CHKDSK	82
/H switch in XCOPY	70
/L switch in CHKDSK	84
/M switch in BACKUP	63
/M switch in CHKDSK	85
/M switch in RESTORE	66
/M switch in XCOPY	69
/N switch in RESTORE	66
/P switch in CHKDSK	85
/P switch in RESTORE	66
/P switch in XCOPY	69
/R switch in CHKDSK	85
/R switch in XCOPY	70
/S switch in BACKUP	62
/S switch in CHKDSK	85
/S switch in RESTORE	65
/S switch in XCOPY	69
/T switch in BACKUP	64
/V switch in CHKDSK	82
/V switch in XCOPY	69
/W switch in XCOPY	70

A

Access light	17
Access time	3
Active partition	32
Actuator	3
ALT key character entry	71
Amstrad PC1512	12, 14, 22, 24
ANSI screen driver	75
APPEND	51
Applications	40, 47
Archive attribute	60
AT case rails	13
AT controller	8
AT Setup	21
Attributes	88
AUTOEXEC.BAT	33, 49

B

BACKUP	54, 58, 70
BACKUP command	62
Backup copy protected progs	61
Backup disks	67
Backup policy	66
Backup programs	58

Backup	53, 57, 60
Bad tracks	21, 25
Batch file parameters	73
Batch file	47, 50, 68, 76
BIOS	16, 22
Boot sector	87
Booting from hard disk	32
BUFFERS in CONFIG.SYS	34
Buffer	25

C

Cache	16
CHDIR	43
CHKDISK	82
Clean Room	2
CONFIG.SYS	33, 46
COUNTRY	63
Command tail	73
Computer auction	14
Controller card	4, 8, 10, 13, 16
CP/M 86	20, 32
Cylinders	20

D

DAT backup	58
Data leads	11
Date formats	63
DEBUG	22
DIR command	37
DISKCOPY	54
Directory entries	88
Disk capacity	1
Disk drive bay	4
Disk drive	2
Disk sizes	5
DOS 4	1
DOS disk structure	87
DRDOS	1, 24, 26, 29, 30, 53, 59, 63, 86
DTP Files	1
dBASE III plus	78
dBASE IV	1

E

EISA	15
Electrical noise	9
ESDI	10
Extended partition	30
External drive	4

F

FAT	31, 53, 87
FDISK	23, 26, 29
FILES in CONFIG.SYS	34
File fragmentation	53, 83
Fitting a disk	13
Floating drive	46
FORMAT	30
Format program	22

G

GEM 40, 54, 75
GOTO batch file command 81

H

Hard card 4, 6, 17
HDFORMAT 23
Heads 20
Height of drives 6
Heirarchical filing system 37
High-level format 19, 30

I

IBM backup format 59
IF ERRORLEVEL 81
IF EXIST 76, 80
IF NOT 80
IF string 80
IF . . . GOTO 81
Interface standards 10
Interleave factor 25
Interleave 9, 16, 24

L

LABEL 71
LASTDRIVE 46
Log file for BACKUP 64
Logical drive 20, 24, 30
Lost clusters 82
Low-level format 19

M

MCA 15
MFM 9
MKDIR 42
MS-DOS 3.2 63
MS-DOS 4.00 24
MS-DOS 22, 26, 29

N

Norton Utilities 53, 59
Number of disk drives 7

O

Operating system 19
Overheating 14

P

PATH 47, 77
Partition size 29
Partitioning 19, 26
PC Tools De Luxe 53, 59, 84
PC-DOS 22, 29
Platter 5
Power consumption 5
Power plug 7
Power supply rating 7
Primary partition 30

R

RESTORE 54, 58, 61, 65
Removable hard disk 4
Renaming in batch files 75
RLL 9
RMDIR 44
ROM BIOS 8, 21, 33
Root directory 37, 47, 87
Rotation speed 2

S

SASI 12
SCSI II 11
SCSI 10
Screening 6, 14
Sector 86
Sectors 20, 23
Sidekick 54
Slots 15
ST412 10
ST506 10
Stepper motor 3
SUBST 46, 78
Subdirectories in BACKUP 62
Subdirectory creation 42
Subdirectory levels 41
Subdirectory 37, 40, 51, 55, 78, 88
System configuration 33
System files 30, 38

T

Tape streamer 57
Terminating resistor pack 12
TREE 45
Tracks 20, 23
Twist in data cable 12

U

UNIX 20, 32
Utility programs 39

V

Vibration 15
VOL 61
Voice-coil 3
Volume label 71

W

WINDOWS 40, 54
Wildcards 62

X

XCOPY 68
XDEL 53
XENIX 32
Xebec 11, 22
XT controller 8